Dorothy Ringling

Ethelwyn Wetherald

Copyright © 2004 by Dorothy Rungeling
All rights reserved

Published by Dorothy Rungeling
Design, layout and cover by Dorothy Rungeling
Printed in Canada by Premier Impressions Inc.

ISBN 0-9731800-2-1

No part of this publication may be reproduced
or transmitted in any form, by any means,
electrical, mechanical, photocopying
recording or otherwise
without the prior written permission
of the author

Life and Works of

ETHELWYN

WETHERALD

1857 – 1940

With a selection of her poems and articles

by
Dorothy W. Rungeling

ACKNOWLEDGMENTS
✧✧✧✧✧

My sincere thanks to:

Mary Lamb for her excellent proof reading.

Welland Tribune for any articles which may have appeared in their newspaper many years ago.

The people who inspired me to write this book so they could learn more about Ethelwyn Wetherald.

Table of Contents

✧✧✧✧✧

Ethelwyn the Poet..	7
Sam and Sally's Romance...	12
A New Family Arrives...	17
Ethelwyn the Person..	23
Rockwood to Pelham via Philadelphia.........	31
Schooling on American Soil.......................................	36
A Taste of Women's Lib?................................	41
Ethelwyn the Journalist..	46
Back to Tall Evergreens...	54
The House in the Trees...	64
Ethelwyn the Mother..	68
Who Was Ethelwyn?..	76
Tragedies..	81
The Party...	89
1940...	95
Selection of Poems....................... 101	
List of Wetherald's Books 131	

INTRODUCTION
✧✧✧

    I have tried to give as true a picture of Ethelwyn Wetherald as possible. Am I biased? Of course I am. If not I would not be a very good daughter. Yes, there were times when Ethelwyn was not the angel that she was thought to be by her friends. She was human and had good reason if she sometimes displayed negative emotions. She had many family problems which she did not share with anyone. But I never heard her speak negatively about anyone. She may have made little jokes about someone's unusual traits but she always impressed on me: "No matter how bad a person may be—there is ALWAYS something good to be found in him."

    My childhood playmates used to look upon Ethelwyn as some sort of saint. She could do no wrong in their eyes and they were sure that when Ethelwyn got to the age where she wanted to leave this earth she would leave, at a time of her own choosing. And perhaps she did that. World War II broke out shortly before her death and she abhorred war. Perhaps she decided that this was the time.

    When her poetry is compared to the modern poetry of today one can see a vast difference in the amount of effort put forth to create it. Whereas today's poetry is a thought put in a format that gives it the appearance of the old poetry, still it does not have the rhyme and metre that the old poetry had. To get the thought, the rhyme and the metre all together perfectly is a work of art. Ethelwyn had the gift to do this.

    I hope that this book will bring back to life the memory of one of Canada's great poets, and make new readers aware that they once had a true celebrity in their midst. It is my hope that Ethelwyn will be celebrated for all she has given to the world and never again left in the darkness of the past.

ETHELWYN THE POET

A gentle breeze, pussy willows breaking out of their hard shells, a bird call, cumulus clouds drifting to nowhere, or the rustle of autumn leaves under foot—and another poem was born. This was Ethelwyn Wetherald.

It seemed that she had a vast storage of verse within, just waiting for the cue to make an exit and become real thoughts in word form, for others to enjoy. From the time she was seventeen in 1874, when she sold her first poem "The Willow Wand", describing the antics of her two younger brothers Lewis and Herbert to *St. Nicholas Magazine* for twelve dollars, until she died just before her 83rd birthday in 1940 she never stopped pouring out her verse.

However, her first fame was won as a journalist when she wrote for several newspapers and magazines on various subjects. All the while she was writing poems but did not have enough for a book until 1895, when *The House of the Trees* was published by Briggs in Toronto.

To Ethelwyn, beauty was everywhere and she had an almost uncontrollable urge to express that beauty in rhyme. Her verse was exquisite, the metre perfect and whether she wrote a sonnet, lyric or just plain verse for children, the rules of classic poetry were followed. As John Garvin a noted writer said:

> Ethelwyn Wetherald is one of the best of Canada's sonnet writers. She has used the most difficult form of the Petrarchan or Italian School, yet the thoughts and lines flow with the same grace and frequency as in her lyrics. This is an unusual achievement. It is seldom one meets with such perfection in word, phrase and line. The thought is invariably original and the expression artistic and lucid. Indeed

Ethelwyn Wetherald's poetry charms and delights all readers, from the University Professor down to the Kindergartner. And this, it seems to me, is the supreme test of genius.

She was acclaimed during her lifetime as one of Canada's greatest and most beloved poets. And she was Pelham's own!

Her verse was chosen by the Department of Education to appear in School Readers, and in 1911 she received a high honour when Sir Wilfred Laurier quoted her poem "My Orders" in the House of Commons.

MY ORDERS

My orders are to fight.
   Then if I bleed, or fail,
Or strongly win, what matters it?
   God only doth prevail.

The servant craveth naught
   Except to serve with might
I was not told to win or lose,–
   My orders are to fight.

When Ethelwyn died she left many letters from admirers of her poetry, some of which she had kept, tied up in a neat bundle with the words on the outside: "KEEP! LETTERS FROM FAMOUS PEOPLE". Along with this was another bundle of letters from a romance she had when young, which had faded into oblivion due to a terrible misunderstanding but many years later was rekindled as a great friendship between the two involved. These letters were destroyed as I knew she would wish them to be.

From the "KEEP" bundle there was a letter from Wilson

MacDonald of great fame, who had boundless admiration for her poetry. The following letter was written to her in 1939 only a year before her death. It not only displays his beautiful penmanship but tells exactly what he thought about Ethelwyn's poetry.

> 1717 Graham Boulevard,
> Town of Mount Royal, P.Q.
> March 1st, 1939
>
> Dear Ethelwyn Wetherald:
>
> I have been ill for two months with neuritis, hence much of my mail has been unanswered during the past two months.
>
> I was very pleased indeed to get your letter. Canada, to my mind, has had only four women poets — Ethelwyn Wetherald, Isabella Crawford, Marjorie Pickthall and Pauline Johnson (in four poems). To a lesser degree (because entirely derivative) Audrey Brown.
>
> You said you would send me some of your recent poetry and I am anxiously waiting to see it.
>
> On January 11th a baby-girl came to the House of MacDonald and we have named her Ahzri Meriden. The nurses at the hospital nicknamed her "Miss Adorable."
>
> I hope the mantle of creation is still upon you and that your days may be long so that the vineyards of Fenwick may never grow lonely for a pure song.
>
> Sincerely,
> Wilson MacDonald.

Another one from the KEEP bundle was from Duncan Campbell Scott, a few lines of which are shown below:

In 1907 Earl Grey, Governor General of Canada, wrote a letter to Ethelwyn to convey to her how much he admired and appreciated her poetry and placed an order with the publisher of her latest book, *The Last Robin*, for 25 copies to give as gifts to his friends.

But she wore her fame too modestly. She did not push her talents as did other writers of her era. A selfless person, she would have been more likely to help publicize someone else's poetry rather than her own. As a result she became all but forgotten. It has been particularly sad that her own community of Pelham, which was home to her for seventy-four years, forgot about her. She was something that not every country had. How many localities have had the fortune of having a resident who was successful as both a journalist and a poet in both Canada and the United States—a person who wrote prose just as easily as she penned her beautiful poems. Pelham and especially Fenwick, which was her postal address, have a right to be very proud.

In 1925 along with other poems by such famous poets as Tennyson, Longfellow, Lowell, Carman, Emerson, whose work appeared in the *Ontario School Readers*, there was Ethelwyn's

"Red Winged Blackbird". It was a great honour to be the first (and only, at that time) woman poet to have her work selected for these school books.

This poem is truly a Pelham poem. Ethelwyn once told me that it came to life one day when she was walking to Fenwick from her farm home, situated on what is now Foss Road. Walking up Cream Street she was approaching Welland Road when she saw a lot of activity in the swampy land to the west side of Cream Street. Flashes of brilliant red almost illuminated the swamp. They were birds—red winged blackbirds! She watched them for a few minutes admiring the beautiful show of red whenever one took flight. All the while there was a poem coming to life in her mind. She hurried home to get it on paper and from then on it was history.

Who is to say where she got her poetical flair from? There is a very interesting and unusual tale of a romance which happened in the 1800s to her maternal grandparents, which could have left its romantic mark on the generations to follow. It is a tale which has been passed from generation to generation and was appealing enough for the *London Free Press* to print an account of it written by Marjorie Cropp in 1967 under the name of "The Irish Cobbler". The following chapter is written using information from Ethelwyn's own story of what happened. It gives a little peek into the past and illustrates some of the hardships and joys of life in the early 1800s.

SAM AND SALLY'S ROMANCE
✧✧✧

Sarah Harris' childhood was spent as was that of most girls in Ireland in the late 1700s—learning how to cook and knit and embroider. When she was six years old in 1792 she made a beautiful "sampler" with her favourite verse neatly embroidered in colour. This sampler is still in existence 212 years later although it has lost most of its colours.

When Sally (Sarah) grew older she was employed by a very well to do Irish family to act as governess to three children. She loved her job but when she became thirty-six years old her life suddenly became a turmoil. In those days a woman of that age was certainly deemed to have become an "old maid" but a man 13 years her junior had started to court her. He was a shoe maker. She was not in the least interested but he refused to give up and go away. His name was Samuel Balls and when he was not making shoes, he was playing his beloved fiddle. Although she did nothing to encourage him and a lot to discourage him, still he kept knocking at her door. She pointed out that he was much too young for her but he would not listen. She told him that she was a Quaker and the Quakers did not believe in mixing religions in marriages. He still did not listen. He had his mind made up that she was the one woman in the world that he wanted to marry and no one was going to change his mind. Age difference was of no concern to him—neither was difference in religious beliefs.

Sally had heard that Sam was not the most industrious person on earth. It was said that Sam had once declared that he would rather play on his fiddle than make the best pair of gold buckled shoes for King George. She brought this to his attention during a heated argument they had, only to get the reply that if she had more music in her soul, she would not be so hard to get along with.

At last Sally as much as told him he was being quite obnoxious. He stormed out stating that he would never come back to the house to see her. He didn't! Instead, he followed her whenever she went out. Sally became sick of the whole thing and felt that she must get away. She told her employers of her problem, packed a trunk and set sail for Canada where her brother had gone to live a few years earlier.

This was quite an undertaking in those days as Canada was still sparsely settled and those hardy souls who ventured here to "homestead" had their lifetime work cut out for them—especially when they settled on farms which in most part were uncleared land. When Sally did not receive any letters from Sam at her new home, she felt that she had herself well hidden in her brother's farm house near Guelph, Ontario.

Across the ocean in Ireland Sam was mourning his loss of the one woman in the world that he truly loved. He worked hard, made more shoes and saved his money and eventually decided to cross the ocean to Canada and find Sally. He was pretty sure of where she was.

It was a six week voyage to cross the ocean. Then he had to get to Guelph, which was in what was called Upper Canada at that time. Once near Guelph he had to find the farm on which he suspected Sally was living. As he walked the many miles hunting for her, he would stop at each house he came to and ask where Sally lived. Finally he found the house. It was just getting dark and the candle lights in the house were flickering—almost as a welcome. His heart must have been pounding as he knocked on the door. When it opened there stood Sally!

No one knows just what transpired during the weeks that followed but Sally evidently decided that perhaps Sam wasn't such a bad catch after all and married him in 1824 as soon as he could build a log cabin for their home.

Her memories of this log cabin were handed down from generation to generation over the years. One of them was the time when Sally was reading by the open window one evening and a wolf stuck his head through the window. Her only means of defense was the burning candle. She picked it up and swiftly stuck it right on the wolf's nose, which sent the animal scurrying back into the dense woods for safety. Another adventure with wolves was remembered and put in story form by Ethelwyn Wetherald, Sally's grand-daughter, many years later:

> Equal to that for interest was the most exciting day of my Mother's life. She with her brother and sister (my uncle and aunt) had visited Aunt Jane, and had carelessly stayed beyond the hour of home coming laid down by Grandfather. "Junie" (my mother) was a fat toddler of four, Auntie was eight and Uncle ten. Early on the homeward walk they heard the sound of wolves.
>
> "What's that noise?" asked the little girl.
>
> "Dunbar's dogs" said the brother, who gave the older girl a significant look. Each grasped a hand of the youngest and rushed along the rough path toward home.
>
> Nearer and nearer came the baleful sounds. The older two were terrified and the little one, being dragged over bush, bog and brier, fallen logs and soaking swamp, cried out that she wasn't afraid of dogs; that she wanted to walk slow. The pack was so near them that they burst into tears, crying out:
>
> "It's wolves!" and flung themselves over the fence which surrounded the cabin, falling exhausted on the step at the open door, as the wolves reached the fence and hesitated before the light within. Grandmother was speechless with thankfulness, but Grandfather took them one by one and gave each of them the hardest spanking they had ever received in all their lives And every slap was simply delicious. A spanking seemed like one of the nicest things in

the world compared with being eaten alive by a lot of famished wolves. Grandmother said:
"Now you'll come home by daylight next time." And they certainly did.

Sally and Sam got along beautifully. Sam couldn't do enough for his darling Sally and Sally began to feel different about Sam's drawbacks. Eventually they had three children, one of whom was Jemima (Junie) born in 1829.

When any neighbourhood event took place such as building a barn or doing some other momentous farm job which necessitated a lot of manpower, Sam always took his violin with him and played the old Irish jigs and hornpipes during rest periods. It was such a contradiction to the way Sally liked to live. She insisted on remaining the gentle Irish lady that she was brought up to be. She retained the ritual of having "tea" every afternoon at five o'clock which was a highlight in the little community of farms as no one else dreamed of such a ceremonious event in their homes. Her teapot, teacup and saucer were treasures which were kept in the family long after she was gone. I remember as a child seeing them safely tucked away in the cupboard. I was allowed to touch them if I was very careful.

Sam was working hard, clearing land and planting crops but money was very scarce. Sally had been teaching neighbouring children in her own home but now she had been requested to teach in a school "up Yonge Street." some miles away. It would mean being away for months at a time but she decided that it was the right thing to do and accepted. With three children they needed the money. When she came home to her family every six months or so she always brought clothing and other gifts for the whole family. Sam would remark that she was "spending her money like a drunken sailor" as he looked at her with the never-ending love still shining in his eyes.

The family was brought up to know how to work. One

year Sam entered the Guelph Fall Fair vying for first prize for the best bushel of wheat. It was a long, tedious job getting it ready as Sam and the children sat at a table and picked over the thousands of kernels of wheat one by one, choosing only the full, good-looking kernels to put in the bushel basket for the fair. He won first prize. The whole family rejoiced and probably celebrated this great occasion with home made fun like a "taffy pull".

At last the farm began to make enough money for Sally to resign her job of teaching and come home to be with her family. Sam was overjoyed.

A NEW FAMILY ARRIVES
✧✧✧

Healaugh, Swaledale, England.   Photo by Les Smith

It was 1834 and a new family moved into the area— the family of John Wetherald, a Quaker, who had been the village butcher in a peaceful little village named Healaugh, in Swaledale, County of York, England.

With its stone fences, hills and dales and the sheep pasturing in the quiet fields it was, and still is, a beautiful setting but evidently the call of the wild reached John and he set sail with one son and one daughter to come to Canada and homestead.

His trip was not easy. After a six week journey over the Atlantic they finally reached New York. They then took a steamer to Albany and on the following day they traveled by rail to Schenectady and then by coach to Utica. They left here by

"The Stage" at four o'clock one morning and traveled 24 hours to cover the eighty miles to Oswego, N.Y. From there they boarded a schooner and sailed 70 miles to Kingston, Ontario. Here they were stuck for a week for lack of any means of transportation. But on April 7th they left Kingston by steamer and arrived the next day at Toronto, which at that time was named York.

Here John left his two children, presumably with relatives, and took a steamer to Burlington Bay with a friend also from England. From Burlington they walked to Dundas and on another 30 miles to Guelph. He purchased a 100 acre farm for $250.00 plus another $275.00 to be paid in nine annual instalments to a government agency in Toronto. Only one acre of the 100 acre farm had been cleared. The family had a monumental job ahead of them.

The next year, 1835, he sent for four more of his children. One of them, a son named William who was fifteen years old, had received education in England at Ackworth, a Quaker boarding school. William was about nine years old when he was sent to Ackworth and evidently didn't relish the idea. He wrote a little poem which described his feelings about it—a verse which shows he likely needed what Ackworth could offer him. The poem was found over a hundred years later. In William's handwriting with its many spelling errors, it read:

> I have entered thee for Ackworth
> Whas all my father said
> And terning quickley from the door
> he thought hed kilt me dead.

However, it turned out to be the right thing for his father to have done. It was at Ackworth that William discovered that he loved to learn even though he had to learn some pretty hard lessons. One in particular was penned by his daughter Ethelwyn, in her collection of family stories.

The first meal Father had at Ackworth would have delighted Jiggs, as it consisted of corned beef and cabbage. He ate the beef and left the vegetable. At supper the same plate was set before him with the cabbage still upon it. He considered this an error on the part of the table setter. At breakfast the same portion of cabbage with its vitamins looking a trifle discouraged, still held the center of the plate like a shipwrecked sailor waiting to be rescued. Then a fellow pupil whispered to him:

"If I were thee, I'd eat that cabbage. It doesn't improve with age."

The new pupil ate the cabbage but never to my knowledge tasted that vegetable again.

By the time he had emigrated to Canada he knew that he wanted to be well-educated. But now, being on a farm in the middle of nowhere, there was no place for him to further his education. With a farm to clear and get producing so they could make the yearly payments, they couldn't afford to send him to a school which cost money, so he decided to educate himself. At the age of 15 he started making axe handles which he sold to farmers around the country. The money he got was spent on pen, ink and books. He studied mathematics, algebra, geometry, calculus, trigonometry, surveying, literature, ancient and English history and languages—everything that he needed to know to make a place for himself in this new world. He also bought a bible as he had a keen interest in religion. However, he still had to help with the farm work , so he studied at night by the light of a candle, after the farm work was finished. He was also known to have given the oxen with which he was working an unnecessary rest in the field while he sat under a shade tree and worked out a problem in trigonometry. He got only four hours of sleep each night for seven years, but he mastered every subject and finally was ready to go out and pass it on to others. He got a job teaching at a small country school near Guelph. It was a four mile walk each way every day.

In the meantime he had come to know Sam and Sally's daughter Jemima, who was 9 years his junior and even when she was a little girl he said that when she grew up he would marry her. He did, in 1846 when he was 26 and she was 17.

The marriage had its ups and downs, particularly during the first few years. Many years later Ethelwyn wrote about her father and mother and their differences:

> The hardest part of my parents' wedded life was in the first year. To speak the plain truth my sympathies are completely with them both.
> Here was a young man whose ambition was whipped to white heat by the semi-scorn of friends and relatives, who detected in him that sense of superiority which we are all inclined to feel a little intolerable. He walks four miles to the village school, his cold lunch with him, comes home tired and hungry to find an empty house. No sign of wife, no smell of dinner. She is out wandering the woods and hills with a young relative—her husband's ten year old nephew, of similar tastes. The fire is out. Pangs of indigestion, assisted by pardonable irritation set in. What to do? He feels as one who has adopted an irresponsible child. Finally he goes to Aunt Jane's house and lays the case before Uncle John.

Soon he decided to start his own school, a boarding school for boys. He advertised his new venture in the GuelphAdvertiser and soon had a small group of boys. He taught them in a log cabin school in Rockwood, Ontario. In 1851 the class was growing and he moved to a story and a half structure which he named Rockwood Academy. Things went well but soon he again needed larger quarters. By 1854 he had built a stately four-storey stone structure of Georgian design. This building is still standing today in 2004 and is an historic site. It contained rooms for two or three extra teachers, classrooms, and nine dormitory rooms on the fourth floor to house up to 50 students. The family quarters were on the third floor and contained five bedrooms for the family as well as two extra ones for the help.

The kitchen, where the cook Big Old Ann reigned, as well as the boys' dining room, was in the basement. There was also an infirmary, a housekeeper and seven extra women helpers as well as a man to do heavier work outside.

William Wetherald had only one requisite for a prospective pupil. That was knowledge of the English alphabet. He would do the rest. It would seem that he had initiated a giant task and soon he had more applications than he could handle. Tuition was $12.00 a month in the English subjects but French, Latin and Greek were $1.00 a month extra. This fee covered room and board and the school instruction. He turned out students who became quite famous, such as J.J. Hill, the railroad magnet, Arthur Sturgis who later became Premier of Ontario and Sir Adam Beck of Hydro fame. Parents were kept well informed by letter of the advancement of their children. William always kept copies of these letters, which are now in the University of Guelph Special Collections.

Note: It is interesting to know that most of the movie *Agnes of God* was filmed at Rockwood Academy, which served as a convent in the picture starring Jane Fonda. It is also almost eery when one realizes that Ethelwyn's first name was Agnes and that she was born in or very near the room where the baby in the film was born.

Rockwood Academy 1980 after restoration by Josef Drenters

Wm. Wetherald family 1862 - Ethelwyn far right

ETHELWYN THE PERSON
✧✧✧

On April 26, 1857, in a sunny room facing south, overlooking the peaceful Rockwood countryside, the sixth of eleven children was born to Jemima and William, with a midwife in attendance as was the custom in those days. No one even dreamed of it then but this baby was to become internationally famous before the century was out. To Jemima and William she was just another blessing that had come to them. She was named Agnes Ethelwyn.

The stately Rockwood Academy was well remembered by Ethelwyn in later years, as she described her mother's sewing room, the cook named Big Old Ann, and the school boys "thundering" down the stairs from the class rooms upstairs, to the dining room in the basement. One of her most vivid recollections of her early home was that of the school boys racing down the stairs at lunch time. If she happened to be near the stairs she was inevitably swept up by one of the boys and held high in the air. It was no doubt a very friendly, loving and playful gesture on the part of the boys but when Ethelwyn told this story, one could notice a trace of hostility. She was her own person even at this early age and resented someone tossing her about. Perhaps it was such unpleasant memories that kept her from visiting the old home in the next century. I don't remember her ever intimating that she would like to go to Rockwood and see the old academy. Her own words indicate that she was a very lonely and serious child. She once wrote:

"There has been much joy and laughter in my life; yet I can recall no occasion when I laughed outright in my early years."

From being very close to Ethelwyn I gleaned a lot about how she felt about herself when a child. She was the oldest of the two living daughters so, as it so often happens, she had to leave center stage for her younger sister Jane. While Ethelwyn was not considered as having a striking appearance as a child, Jane was plump, blue eyed, rosy cheeked, playful and cuddly. While Jane was full of ambition, Ethelwyn was considered to be the frail child of the family so found herself immersed in books all by herself, while the other children were having fun playing. It would seem that as many children do, Ethelwyn felt that she was not beautiful, could not compete with her sister Jane and put herself down. This often left her in the house reading such grown-up books as Shakespeare instead of enjoying the company of other children. It is ironical that in later years Ethelwyn "the frail one" turned out to be the one who nursed many of her brothers and her sister through illnesses and death and outlived them all. In maturity she was held in esteem by her friends and acquaintances. Her knowledge and talent far outweighed that of her sister Jane and she at last came into her own.

In her later years Ethelwyn penned her memories of her early life at Rockwood, which painted a picture of what life and diets were like in the mid 1800s:

> My first impressions of food were received in my father's boarding school, Rockwood Academy. At the head of the long dining table sat the Principal; at his right the youngest child—three year old Charlie in his high chair. At his left and as much in need of parental oversight, was the eldest daughter. Then came Mother, little sister Jane, the brothers, two assistant teachers, followed by two or three dozen teen age boys from all parts of the country. As Wordsworth somewhere says of a field of cattle, we were "forty feeding as one."
>
> Hills and houses look large in retrospect and certainly the table was pretty well cleared when we rose from it, but it

seemed to me among the steaming vapours of huge platters of beef with high piled potatoes and turnips or plenteous roast pork with cabbage or beans, that there was a most unmerciful amount of food. My unfortunate peculiarity being that I was a dyspeptic first and a child afterwards, not a soul at the table shared my views except little Charlie, who promptly threw his plate over his head when its contents displeased him. What with keeping one eye on his pupils and the other on Charlie's plate and my pinafore pocket (in which I tried to secrete "large chunks of fat as big as my two thumbs") father was a busy man at meal times. He himself ate little but never missed a meal. As a rule the scholars were too hungry to be mischievous. One boy devised a method of handling his knife in a way that landed a piece of butter on the ceiling, to which it adhered. But he took small pride in the achievement, afraid of the wrath to come.

Although a light eater, father delighted in seeing all around him swell visibly, not only family and pupils, but every horse, cow, cat, dog and chicken on the place. So plump little Jane sat next to Mother, a coveted privilege—while I, between the frequent attacks of my sire's left elbow while he was carving meat, kept wondering whether it was better to bear the unappetizing ills I had, or fly from others I knew too much of, the alternative being a dose of Epsom salts, castor oil or at least a big spoonful of "brimstone and treacle".

Only one flight of that sort was successful. That was when at the age of five, I refused to take the spoonful of castor oil presented by Mother. According to the slang of today I "couldn't take it." I flew into the kitchen, then into the dining room, upstairs into a bedroom where I hid under the bed covers. Little Janie followed Mother, who, flushed and indignant with unwanted exercise, placed the spoon carefully on a chair, while she started to deal with me single handed. It wasn't difficult for a lean lively child to roll across the bed or run around to the other side to elude solicitous maternal hands. At length my small sister, wearying of the fray, picked up the spoon and, without a shudder licked it clean. "There Mother, it's gone now. We don't need to fight any more." Warfare was not renewed. "Naughty child! I've a great mind to tell thy father." I knew she wouldn't. Janie was regarded as half martyr, half idiot. For me the sense of victory was delicious. I had "killed my bear"—was a conqueror.

Alas, it is only she who is down who need fear no fall. The very next day, stung by the sight of Mother, sitting down in mid morning to a light lunch of biscuit and beer (prescribed as a tonic by our physician) I insisted on having my share. It was incredible that Mother should be seen eating anything without giving "Benjamin's portion" to her offspring. So I would not take no for an answer. The result was I have never since touched a drop of spirituous liquor. I know what it tastes like. Also I have consistently avoided the phrase "I told you so!" I know what it sounds like.

To return to the dining room which was run on strictly economical principles. Breakfast oatmeal was bought by the barrel and required hours of cooking. Suet puddings were thinly populated with raisins and those of rice, baked in milk pans, were not conspicuous for fruit. Apples cost money so we seldom saw them except when hiding coyly in the bulgy depths of deep apple pie. Shallow pies "kivered, unkivered and cross barred" sometimes held dried apples stewed into smoothness and flavoured with discretion, but they were more likely to contain rhubarb, pumpkin, black or red currants, wild thimble berries or green gage plums from our own plum trees. The prickly gooseberry made its appearance as gooseberry fool. We saw oranges at Christmas. But there was a lamentable lack of salad vegetables. Lettuce, if passed around would provoke the comment "I don't eat grass." Cucumbers were viewed with alarm, a favourite quip of the period being "Don't eat too many Q-cumbers, they will W-up!"

Tomatoes, known as love apples, were held in similar esteem as toad stools. Raw cabbage chopped to pin head size, sharp with vinegar and hot with pepper was understandable but cooked food was preferred. The stalwart young Canadians who boarded with us looked not upon beet greens unless they were red and gave their colour in the dish. Dandelions were for medical use only. People who ate "lamb's quarter" (a palatable green, growing wild in spring) were considered too poor to have the kind of lamb's quarter that has to be carved. Carrots we seldom saw on the table, probably for the good reason that no one would eat them. Was there ever a boy on earth who hungered after a boiled carrot? If vigorous, he might eat it raw and enjoy the flavour all the more if forbidden. Creamed carrots has an appealing sound but if the "cream" consists of flour and watery milk—no thank you.

Vitamins, calories and protective foods were unheard of. No one implored us to eat what was good for us, nor wept, as I saw a young mother weep lately, because her little boy refused to finish up his "nice spinach." Pupils and family alike followed the good old rule of Methuselah, who ate what he found on his plate with no immediate fatal results.

Not that health was disregarded. It wasn't brooded over or talked about. As with colts and calves you were expected to be well. If not well you were sick.

Had it not been for abundant raspberries growing wild around neighbouring hills and thickets we should have sorely missed the vitamins of which we had never heard. When I insisted on accompanying Big Old Ann (the housekeeper) with her satellites, slim young Annie O'Connor, Fanny Best and Margaret Knowles and perhaps our nurse Mary Edwards and "the missus" as mother was called—on their twice a year pilgrimage after berries, I was given a small tin cup and told to fill it for Janie. We took a lunch basket along and returned at night fall with brimming pails, but the little tin cup was empty. Selfish tyke was what they called me but self preservation had warned me that this was probably my last chance of devouring lusciously ripe berries unadulterated with muscovado sugar, pound for pound. Jane could forage for herself.

Whatever advantage I took of my baby sister reverted to my own head. Invariably she "got even." There was the incident of the plum tree, not a green gage. The fruit was a dark delicious red, egg sized and egg shaped. Father had warned us to leave that tree alone. Accordingly, forsaking all other trees we clove only to it, playing under it in the hope that some over ripe specimen might drop. At last one day when the coast was apparently clear, I induced an older brother to boost me up. A dozen plums, bluish, reddish, enchantingly delectable, high above me. One would never be missed. My mouth watered profusely. Then turned to ashes. Janie was calling up in a stage whisper:

"Come down. Somebody is watching you."

And the biggest plum so nearly in my grasp. Well at least I could say in my defense that I hadn't touched one. I descended hastily, bruised, scratched and trembling, for the peculiar emphasis my sister had put on the word "somebody" led me to expect an interview with our irate sire. Looking around in every direction as I brushed tell tale twigs from my clothing I demanded who was watching me. Little Jane smiled sweetly, cocked her head like a robin and said:

"God."

Ethelwyn was a very quiet, unassuming person, always thinking of others, always able to put herself in the other person's place and always willing to help. It is an honour for me, Ethelwyn's adopted daughter, to pass on memories of her life - her conquests and her tragedies, during the eighty-two years of her fascinating time on earth.

Ethelwyn was five feet, five inches tall and of slight stature, although she stated that in her thirties she weighed one hundred and thirty pounds. Her slight stature was more than outweighed by her indomitable spirit and she overcame many tragedies during her life that would have been too much for the average person to bear. She was a very gentle, unselfish and loving person. Her hair was dark brown in younger years. Photographs show her wearing a hair style that would pass as "up to date" today, but my remembrance is that she parted it in the centre and drew it back into a "bun" in the back. She wanted to keep up with the times and at one time quite late in life, decided to have her hair "bobbed", much to the disapproval of some of the family members.

As she grew older, so did her wish to remain "up to date". She wanted to be able to converse with the younger generation in their language and made quite a stir one day when she, in her 70s and impatient with someone's tardiness, exclaimed:

"Oh come on, put your foot on it!"

It took a few moments for her audience to realize that she meant "step on it" which was the phrase of the day to hustle things along. Of course this brought forth peals of laughter from my friends and me, but she took it all as good fun, probably making a mental note to brush up on her modern phrases.

She once shocked some gentle lady friends who were in for afternoon tea. The topic of conversation had touched on prize fighting. It was almost a unanimous decision by the ladies that prize fighting was animal-like and should be abolished, when Ethelwyn spoke up saying that she was not against it. It was certainly not characteristic of her gentle lady-like make-up, but her point was that if people wanted to participate and it was legal, it should be allowed—it was a changing world and without change we do not grow. I rather think that she was just enjoying a good debate. She had an abhorrence of indecision. Often she remarked that "it is better to make the wrong decision than to make no decision."

Ethelwyn received most of her early education at home. From her description of her father, it would be impossible not to have a great deal of his knowledge rub off on her. William, contrary to most beliefs of that day, was emphatic that girls should have the same level of education as boys and he ensured that his two daughters did. He was deeply involved in religion and later became a minister for the Quaker church. Part of the Quaker belief was that there should be no discrimination between the sexes regarding privileges. This deep belief was also instilled in his children, who were faithful members of the church and perhaps, later on, this was the source of Ethelwyn's "feminist views".

Ethelwyn was an avid reader, even as a child. By the time she was fifteen she had read all of Dickens and when she reached twenty she had read all of Shakespeare. Later in life when asked who her favourite writers were, she stated that in her teens she was fond of Emerson, Carlyle and Mathew Arnold.

"The New England poets and essayists Holmes and Lowell always delighted me."

Ethelwyn at age 15

ROCKWOOD TO PELHAM VIA PHILADELPHIA
✧✧✧

In 1864 the Wetherald family was to make a big change. William had been approached by Haverford College, a Quaker boarding school near Philadelphia, to take the position of superintendent. As much as he loved his academy in Rockwood, he felt that the new position would be better for him and his family. He sold his beloved school and moved the whole family to Philadelphia, Pennsylvania. It was here that still another son, Fred, was born in 1865.

Ethelwyn wrote in her memoirs:

> Haverford College was set in a lawn of sixty beautifully manicured acres. Every flower was in its place, the grass properly repressed at regular intervals, and even the beautiful old trees, artistically pruned, had almost forgotten that the groves were God's first temple. Yes, it was attractive. It was all so perfectly trained, so well behaved.

The family remained in Philadelphia only until 1866. William was accustomed to his own method of teaching which had proven highly successful in his own school, but now he was under the orders of the elders who governed the school and he found he could not cope with denying his own principles, so he resigned and returned to Canada. Ethelwyn explains the parting:

> Certainly my father was well liked by the rest of the faculty, but some of his methods gave them uneasiness. They were diplomats; he was a "rugged individualist" the founder of his own Academy, maker of his own rules and resolute upholder of the theory that every man's life should

have for its objective devotion to duty, aided by definiteness of purpose and sound common sense. So with regrets, with affection, with the kindest feelings on both sides, we left Haverford within two years of our arrival.

Since Rockwood Academy was now no longer his, he had to locate elsewhere. Ethelwyn was nine years old and felt that all her dreams had been fulfilled when she and her family settled down in the spot chosen by her father as their future home. It was a fifty-acre farm on the corner of Foss Road and Cream Street in the Township of Pelham, Ontario.

The Quaker community there welcomed them, as William had deep religious convictions and he was happy to accept the role of minister at the Quaker church, which still stands in the year 2004 on Haist Street, in the Town of Pelham. As far as anyone knows he was the first minister in this church. In those days the Quakers did not believe in paying a minister. They wished to have the services administered by someone who was genuinely interested in the gospel and gave his services as an act of love towards his God and congregation. However they kept a watchful eye on their beloved minister and made sure that the family had everything they needed.

According to Ethelwyn, the farm was regarded by her parents as a pretty poor farm, but she was ecstatic about it which no doubt moved her to write the following poem in later years when she reminisced on her childhood:

POVERTY'S LOT

Poverty bought our little lot,
    Flooded with daisy blooms;
Poverty built our little cot
    And furnished all its rooms.

> Yet Peace leans over Labour's chair,
> Joys at the fireside throng,
> While up and down on Poverty's stair
> Love sings the whole day long.

In 1870 Ethelwyn was to have another brother, Lewis, and the last child, Herbert was born in 1872, a total of 11 children, two of whom had died. Ethelwyn was by now fifteen years old and the new baby was very special to her. Little did she know at that time that Herbert would be the one brother with whom she would spend the most of her life. The joy of living on the farm was expressed by Ethelwyn many years later:

> Thus at the age of nine, for the first time in my life I found myself living not in an institution, but in our own private, individual home, just as other people lived. It was a thrilling thought. For us, no more the thunder of many feet descending the stairs at noon or recess, nor any more the sensation of dwelling in an alien male community, inspected or ignored by foreign eyes, among those with whom we could not possibly have anything in common. The new home seemed to be regarded by our elders as a sorry looking farm but it brought great gladness to us. Its very poverty gave a sense of richness. The house was at the end of a long lane, guarded by the "far gate" and the "near gate". What a wealth of privacy! We could go barefoot–the girls as well as boys. And then the apples lying on the ground as thickly almost as when they were buds on the trees! Only cider apples, most of them, but the beauty of a cider apple tree is that its fruit has a different flavour from that of any other apple tree. We recalled the Rockwood days, when if there were no apples left in the bag in the pantry, we were fain to fill the void within with the very parings left after Big Old Ann (the cook) had made her pies, so famished were we for the king of fruits. My eldest brother had been offered a free education at Haverford. This offer was refused by Father, who, being no farmer himself needed a responsible, though only age 15,

man to look after the farm and home. When starting on one of his preaching trips he was wont to say: "Be sure and do what Sam tells you to do."

This was no hardship for me. I have never known anyone else who was as scientifically accurate in his estimate of the rights of others as this elder brother. Our father had a burning love of humanity, but Samuel John, sensitively appraised the rights of the person who happened to be near him. Also he had a delightfully active mind. The older boys slept in a large, two-bedded room at the south end of the old house. My sister and I in the next room off the hall, and these innocent bystanders were sorely vexed at being forced to listen to an earnest discussion on woman suffrage, the theory of evolution or the reason nations act as they do. It was a grief to me that we could not agree on the subject of woman's vote. The utmost concession I could obtain was: "Oh, she has a right to vote—that's sure. But I wish she wouldn't use it."

Next to our new home, the greatest source of interest was The Goings On Across the Road. Directly opposite the far gate was a noble piece of timber, many acres in extent and containing some of the highest, handsomest and best developed trees for miles around. Near the centre of this "bush" a large open space was cleared for the use of a camp meeting with its fiery creators; its exultant believers; its doubting Thomases and its shadow-hidden groups of curious on-lookers and in-listeners. These latter were strongly urged to "cast your deadly doings down" which I understand to be a more elegant way of saying "quit your meanness" until it was explained that deadly doings meant highly moral deeds performed with the aim of earning salvation.

None of our family were supposed to attend the Revival Meetings, though I suspect Jim, Will, Charlie and Fred, slipped over without permission to be nearer the curious sights and sounds. But it was a matter of surprise to the exhorters that my father did not attend. He was seated by the open window one midsummer night, reading Charles Kingsley while loud Hallelujah and admonitory shoutings boomed through the otherwise still air, when an attender at the woodland meetings, half demented by an excess of

revival, burst in at the door, yelling at the top of his voice:
"Mr. Wetherald, we are all going straight to Hell!"
My father turned a page of his book then looked up.
"In that case", he said, after a thoughtful pause, "we may as well go quietly."

It is believed that their first house in Pelham was a log cabin, but as soon as finances permitted, the Wetherald family built a house more compatible with the size of their large family. One of the first things they did after getting settled was to plant a row of Norway Spruce trees along the side of the lane from the house to the road, some four hundred feet. They also planted maple trees along the road frontage of approximately a quarter mile. Many of these trees are still standing in the year 2004. Ethelwyn felt that she had at last arrived home and although she moved around during her early life, this farm was always home to her.

The next thing for the family to do was to plant apple trees. Most of the farm was planted in apple orchards and stayed that way until the 1930s. Within a few years harvest time was a busy time, spent in picking, packing and shipping apples by train to purchasers in distant locations. The extra work load at this time of year was to make a huge change in Ethelwyn's life some forty-five years later.

SCHOOLING ON AMERICAN SOIL

Ethelwyn was now to be launched into another era of her life. In 1869 a very well-to-do Quaker family in Buffalo wrote to William Wetherald offering to take one of his daughters into their own home and provide her with schooling. Ethelwyn, being the eldest daughter, was chosen to go. She also attended a girls' school in Union Springs, New York and later Pickering College, in Pickering, Ontario.

During Ethelwyn's stay at the Union Springs Boarding School she experienced a Christmas which stayed in her memory all her life. In 1940 she shared it in a children's column in the *Welland Tribune*. It is a real insight into how life was lived in the 1800s.

Christmas is supposed to be a call from Home Sweet Home, a strengthener and sweetener of domestic ties. Yet one of the pleasantest Christmas holiday seasons of my life was spent at a Friends' Boarding School in Union Springs, on Cayuga Lake, New York State. Eight of us, five boys and three girls, being so far from home that the family purse refused to consider transportation charges, we were destined to spend the holidays together. The Friends' idea being that the way to cure a person of wanting a thing extravagantly is to give it to him in reasonable amounts, there were none of us either boy crazy or girl mad. Sitting opposite to boys at meal time is a great destroyer of glamour and builder-up of companionableness. Miss Pope, the girls' governess, who lived in the village and Elijah Cook the Principal, whose home joined the Seminary, were more than kind; but J. J.

Thomas showed himself a super-man. As a Trustee we were afraid of him; as a reprimander he was to be avoided. But now his great heart is moved to compassion. Poor little demons! So far away from home and mother! So brave and cheerful about it. Why, that girl from Canada had so sore a throat on Christmas Day, she was in the hospital wing, and could no more have eaten a slice of turkey than she could have chewed up her geography cover! Now, what to do about it? He goes into a huddle with himself and presently emerges with a radiant smile. This he conveys to the Girls' Sitting Room, where are collected the homeless eight.

"How would you like to go somewhere?"

We are electrified. The writers of letters to home, drop their pens. The crocheters drop their crochet hooks. The checker players drop their boards. All eyes are on the speaker.

"You might drive my carryall to Blankley Quarterly Meeting next Seventh Day, and return that evening. No teacher would go with you; we can trust you." He glances at my room-mate Mattie Williamson, who nods intelligently, (she later married a Methodist minister) and also at Daniel—I can't recall his name, but a Daniel come to judgement could not be more impeccable. He is about to add the time worn "I am sure you will conduct yourselves in a way that will confer credit etc. etc." but is overpowered by a chorus of young voices, exclaiming, rejoicing, delighting in anticipation. Not that we are crazy over Quarterly Meeting; but to go where we haven't gone, see what we haven't seen, do what we haven't done—that is what youth desires.

As may be surmised, this carryall is not in the first heyday of youth. It is a large, top heavy vehicle, somewhat creaky in the joints and unsteady in the sinews, but otherwise still in the ring. Daniel the Dependable mounts to the driver's seat. Mattie goes with him to do her back seat driving to advantage. Three boys within try to sit by red headed Mate Moore, but Eddie and I see no one but each other. With a shout of acclaim we are off! The horses show signs of life, not to an indecorous extent, the intelligent brutes know they are going to Quarterly Meeting, but they are certainly in motion. Jiggetty jog, jiggetty jog; we laugh and sing and spare not! The wayfaring man in quiet country villages is accosted with: "Does your mother know you're out?" the prevailing gag of the period. The fourteen miles of our pilgrimage are comfortably covered in less than three hours and we arrive in time for meeting, full of self importance.

A tall, wide, hospitable Friend and his fat and smiling wife were evidently apprised of our coming as they took us home with them to dinner. Never before or since have I been confronted with so large and thickly populated a dinner plate. On it reposed three large slices of turkey, two heaping tablespoons of dressing, the same of Irish potatoes mashed, ditto of sweet potatoes, ditto of creamed onions, ditto of mashed turnip, a large amount of cranberries, a sweet pickle and plenteous gravy poured profusely over all. Before seating ourselves our host inquired: "Which is the sick girl? This one? Fat as a match! Couldn't eat her Christmas dinner hey? Well I'll see she eats this one." He seats me next to him. I blush as brightly as the red flannel bandage showing its edge so coyly among the white ruffles at my throat. Having lived on "milk-toast" three or four days, I am not afraid to eat, and my host's hearty "Atta girl!" cheers me on. But at the advent of plum pudding, mince pie and pumpkin pie, enthusiasm wanes!

The short winter day draws quickly to a close. After a trip to the stables to inspect sheep, cows, ducks and chickens, we gather around the organ to sing with hearts and voices. Then we begin to talk of returning. But this we are not allowed to do without a parting lunch of doughnuts and cider. Eddie and I drive most of the way back and do not seriously imperil the lives of the party. We stop at a small hotel to "rest the horses." One of them breathes heavily and the other shows signs of exhaustion. The boys treat us to soda water and we play games and start to dance. Oh that dance! If I live to be a thousand years old I could never forget it! Holding hard to your partner you went tum tumpty tum tum, (two steps to the left) and tumty umty, tum,tum (two steps to the right). Like the earth we have two motions; one on our axis, the other largely interfering with the axises (Goodness! What IS the plural?) We giggle and laugh, bubble and squeak. The landlord looks in, grinning from ear to ear from teeth to toes. Presently he reappears with a large tray bearing eight tall glasses of raspberry vinegar. "This", he observes grandly, " is on the house."

So we all sit and sip and simmer down. Someone remarks that the horses having been watered have now regained their pristine vigour, and we promised J. J. not to be late. We resume our places in the carryall, Mattie and her Chosen One (was it Alf or Davy?) mount to the driver's seat, and we move with conscious propriety through the quiet Main Street of Union Springs. Suddenly there is a jerk, a pause, a scraping, scrunching sound. Evidently something untoward has happened. We look out to see the right front wheel moving gracefully away into the ditch, while a broken axle drags on the ground. We all alight, villagers gather round and advice is freely given. The horses are not alarmed. Probably this is not the first time they have been compulsory witnesses of a similar scene. After some consultation, four of us start on the uphill walk to the school. One boy remains to guard the horses and three are sent to "explain" to J. J. We feel sorry for the "explainers" but they report next day that the sterling old gentleman blamed no one but himself. One of nature's noblemen was old J. J. Thomas.

Attaining her education in both the United States and Canada gave Ethelwyn an unusual insight into the politics of both countries. This interest was kept alive for the rest of her life and she could discuss the politics and economics of both countries with anyone.

Although only seven years old she gathered up a lot of memories during her residence at Haverford. One of them was the assassination of President Lincoln. The train bearing his body came into Philadelphia on April 22, just four days before her eighth birthday. She tells the story in her own words:

The tragic death of Lincoln was impressed on memory by a nation-wide sadness, intensified by the presence of our father, bowed in grief, and by the sight of the black-draped funeral train, moving with passionate slowness past the college grounds. It was horror and heartache made visible. Jim and Will, Janie and I watched it pass, and felt our spirits heavy and the beautiful April morning darkened by the sorrow of millions of mourning hearts.

Even though she wrote the following poem many years later, this memory must have had something to do with it:

THE VOICE OF LINCOLN

The still, small voice that spoke to Lincoln
    Sounds over Europe's troubled field
Stronger than the thunder of cannon
    Something of God that will not yield.
Rising out of tumult and torture
    Desolation, famine and dearth
Saying Government by the people
    Of the people and for the people
Shall not perish from this earth.

A TASTE OF WOMEN'S LIB?
✧✧✧

When Ethelwyn was in her mid-teens her father had been given a printing press as a gift. He had no idea of how to use it, but managed to get a job for Ethelwyn with the *Welland Tribune* so that she could learn how to set type and then teach him. Many years later in the 1930s she wrote about her experience in a contribution to the "Patty Perkins Column" which appeared in the *Welland Tribune*:

An old friend reminds me that my first contribution to a newspaper was written in the Welland Tribune office. That is true. But any reporting I did then was all in the day's work. My job in Welland in the early seventies (1870s) when I was in my "teens" was to set type. At that time my father had been presented with a small printing outfit which neither he nor I had been able to use, and it was decided that I should go to Welland and learn to set type. I went the more willingly because I had been reading "Views Afoot" by Bayard Taylor, an American author, who had started almost penniless for Europe, and had paid his way by odd jobs of type-setting at local printers along the route, and later by sending accounts of his travels to his home paper. An ideal career! But to follow in Bayard's footsteps required a knowledge of printers' ink.

At that time the Tribune office was reached by an outside stairway, topped by a loose jointed door with a tremendous capacity for banging. My employer Mr. J. J. Sidey, was reticent and considerate. Though apparently less than thirty, he was spoken of (behind his back) as The Old Man. I never knew him to lose his temper or raise his voice, not even when berated by a door banging subscriber or (worse still) advertiser, loud with his story of wrong. Mr.

Sidey's brother Sam was a reporter, and another brother Herbert worked at a case near me. It was rumoured that Sam Sidey received $10.00 a week and George Wells who worked the press got $8.00. I revered these giants of finance, and was proud indeed when I was given $3.50 as my weekly wage. After paying $2.00 for board to Mrs. William Bald, I had $1.50 to salt down for my European trip. "The thoughts of youth are long, long thoughts."

Mr. Bald had a store near the corner of North and Main Streets, and his only daughter May, was the first girl graduate of Toronto University. May and I were (and are) fond of each other. Her little brother Billy (in later years, W. F. Bald, school inspector) seeing our heads close together in eager converse, used to call us The Two-Headed Woman.

I never reached the smooth, even swiftness of hand attained by my fellow workers but I enjoyed life with them. There was one alert, upstanding, fair haired little fellow called Bobby Young, who swept the floor and scrubbed the rollers with as much energy as he banged the door—which is high praise. One noon hour when the boys were skirmishing around the composing room and I was coming up the outside steps, I heard Bobby exclaim: "Stop your racket. Here comes the Thin Space." Whom do you suppose he could have meant? I wish I knew what became of Bobby.

Patty Perkins (the pen name for Mrs. Stewart McInnis of Welland) who ran a children's column in the Tribune in the 1930s brought the above article to the attention of George Wells, who remembered Ethelwyn very well and spoke highly of her. He wrote this reply to Patty Perkins who then published both letters:

> We knew Miss Wetherald quite well as we were shop mates together and we liked her as she appealed to us as an angel among "Printers Devils." As she says, Bobby Young dubbed her "The Thin Space." As we remember the young lady, she was tall and slight and straight and of a graceful figure—in these modern times we would class her

among the "Gibson Girls" by that famous artist.

It would seem that even at this early age, by taking the job at the Tribune, Ethelwyn proved a point regarding equality between sexes, although I am sure she had no idea that she was pioneering anything that was to come to life in such a poignant manner as it has in this century. Although she was very feminine, she always held her ground when it came to discussing the subject of women's independence. It was the custom then for women to press their husbands' pants and clean their shoes, but she stolidly stuck to her viewpoint and would never do either of these chores for her brothers.

Ethelwyn was the perfect lady but at the same time she believed that women should be able to attain anything that they wanted. This trait must have had much to do with Ethelwyn's life, as she held positions usually held by men in the literary world. In one of her regular columns in the *Globe* she wrote the following :

DISCUSSING THE EQUALITY OF MEN AND WOMEN

The difficulty arises from the old notion as false as it is old, that a bad man is better than a bad woman. No amount of tears and protestations, it is said, will prevent two and three from making five, whether the calculation is made by a man or a woman.

It is equally true that a sin in the weaker sex can never be a weakness in the stronger sex. I am not condoning the offense, but whatever the degree or kind of stone throwing indulged in by society, let those who have equally sinned receive an equal share.

Ethelwyn once reminisced on her first experiences as a free lance-writer for a newspaper when she was quite young:

My first experience as a free lance writer for a newspaper was distinctly encouraging I was living with my two brothers in St. Paul, Minnesota and we spent most of our summers at a lake nearby. Some phases of lakeside life interested me and I wrote an account of them which I took to the editor of the Pioneer Press, a quiet dignified man who motioned me to a chair while he read it. I felt very stiff and prim, wishing for escape. Presently he laughed and then he laughed again. It was an agreeable sound which turned all the pins and needles in my chair into a flowery bed of ease. All he said was, "Human interest–that's your line."

The column article appeared the following Saturday and so did the $4.00 payment. I can't remember what was done with either, but that (to me) novel phrase "human interest" has stayed with me ever since.

Some author had previously told me to look in my heart and write. This meant that I should look into other people's hearts and write. It's a good plan to do both. There's a lot of interesting scenery in other people's hearts. The hearts of parents are packed to the brim with anxiety for their children and pride in them. The hearts of children fly in a hundred different directions "like sparks in burnt up paper". The heart of every editor is filled not only with a wish to express his own convictions, but also with a deep desire to please his readers–please them so much that they will multiply endlessly, and never borrow his paper from the neighbours again.

The second editor of a western journal to whom I went, with a would-be contribution, had his feet on the desk, his hat on his head. He brought his feet down but the hat though twitched once or twice, proved irremovable. He also laughed appropriately but declined the article. What he wanted was a society reporter, would I do that? I hesitated for I loved the evenings home with my brothers. "Why it's easy" he urged. "All you have to do is go to parties and say the ladies looked lovely in their chiffons and velvets. They'll cluster around like bees especially if you give them the sugar and spell their names correctly."   But I didn't go to the door when Opportunity knocked. That was an error. Next to being interested in what concerns others, a young writer should be glad to do what needs to be done, whether distasteful or not. Every experience helps to enlarge our knowledge of life.

Ethelwyn Wetherald

ETHELWYN THE JOURNALIST
❖❖❖

In the 1880s Ethelwyn was getting a lot of recognition for both her articles and her poetry. She had contributed articles to the Toronto Globe under the nom de plume of Bel Thistlethwaite, her paternal grandmother's name. The editor, John Cameron, was so impressed that he invited her to come to Toronto to be on the staff and write a regular column for his paper, The Globe. Her articles proved her prowess as a columnist. She could write convincingly about any subject. Her columns covered a remarkably broad range of subjects from poetry, to dieting your way to health, how to lose weight and her abhorrence of funerals. Some of the titles were: "To Lace or Not to Lace"; "Cruelty to Parents"; "Beautiful at Sixty"; "Word on Woman Suffrage"; "Voice Culture for Women".

She had a wealth of knowledge on a myriad of topics. When reading some of these articles, it is amazing to see how up to date she was, by today's definition, on such diverse topics as health, how to decorate your house, whether to choose an Oriental rug "if one could afford it" or be happy with a Wilton, Axminster or Brussels, along with the merits of each type of rug. She always came across as a specialist on the prevailing subject. Her column brought many comments and questions from her readers. Some excerpts from her columns read:

COUNTRY PARLORS AND FURNITURE

The one thing that is more deplorable than the horse hair sofa is the marble topped table. The slippery chair that affords no support to the small of your back, and has no mercy on the large of your back should be turned into kindling wood. One had better have no ornaments at all than to have them matching each other. But there are other crimes against good taste which should be guarded against. One is the practice of covering the parlour walls with family portraits. The proper place for these is in a less public room. Pictures should not be profuse, nor should they be so small that they cannot be clearly seen from the centre of the room. Costly thy pictures as thy purse can buy and let them be hung, not as in old fashioned houses, within a foot or two of the ceiling, but opposite the eye of the observer when he is in a standing position.

Is it necessary to say anything against hair flowers, wax fruit, or any of the other manifold devices for torturing inoffensive materials into unseemly shapes? It does not require a great deal of money to make a home attractive; it does require good taste, good judgment and a great deal of love. It is possible to furnish a house at an enormous outlay and make it a picture of ugliness.

The best advice I can give on the furnishing of a home is to make purchases very deliberately—buying if need be only one thing at a time—and being certain that each thing is just what she wants. It is an expensive way, but it is the way that pays best in the end. Where a chair for instance, or a table is a thoroughly good piece of work, and a cheaper article of the same sort can scarcely be distinguished from it, then it is extravagant to buy the latter, for cheap things are sure to reveal their cheapness sooner or later—generally sooner—and will have to be renewed again and again, while age will only develop the inherent good qualities of the former.

The true test of worth of the writing desk, as is the poem that is written upon it, is the feeling with which it will be regarded a hundred years from now. Time is merciless in his treatment of shoddy material; he delights to deface and destroy it. But what is excellent, Emerson says, is permanent.

Pretense, affectations and deceit must not be permitted in our furnishings. It is a safe rule to distrust overly cheap goods. Silk plush furniture is dear at any price as it soon loses its luster and colour. Chairs covered with a good tapestry of a rather expensive sort will bear the sunshine and wear for years, growing more beautiful with use. Many parlour chairs are so unnecessarily large and heavy that though you may wish your guest to be seated in a comfortable chair, it will be a physical impossibility to hand him one. You may majestically indicate it to him or stand behind it and beckon him with the air of a young mother. If the chin is low, as it probably is, and the visitor is tall and modest, he will not like to fling himself into it with a lordly air and so he will not know what to do with his knees, which will persist in approaching the level of his chin. There are also parlours in which the chairs are so uncomfortable that arriving visitors at once "make a dive" for the sofa like a ship wrecked mariner swimming for the nearest strip of land.

It is a very sensible fashion not to get sets or pairs of anything. There is no reason why a vase or picture frame should match another vase or picture frame and six chairs exactly alike are out of place except in a dining room. As to bookcases—the least objectionable one that I have seen runs across the end of a room at about the height of a chair and projecting two feet from the wall. The broad top makes a delightful place for bric-a-brac and every sort of dainty or precious thing. Between this and the floor there is room for three book shelves which may be protected from dust by small silk curtains attached to a rod with rings. Japanese silk in some of the rich, artistic tints in which it is shown by upholsterers is very pretty for this purpose.

The ornaments of a room should not be "patchy" and profuse. A clutter of elegant trifles continuously reminds one that it is a clutter. Artists never make the mistake of wearying us with the confusion of forms and prefer to give the requisite bits of colour to a room by the means of solid coloured Chinese jars in mustard yellow, or ox-blood red and peacock blue. These are inexpensive and really handsome, as are Japanese vases in sea green. A cultivated taste will at once detect the difference between the merely gaudy and the really beautiful.

Although written 115 years ago, Ethelwyn's suggestions on how to decorate are still as practical today as they were then and could be well worth following. Ethelwyn loved the outdoors and would never permit drapes at the windows because "that would obstruct the beautiful view of the trees against the sky." This was a distinct contradiction of her ideas as published in one of her Globe columns as follows:

CARPETS AND CURTAINS

A floor that is finished with well seasoned chestnut, ash, walnut or yellow pine, will after its nail heads and cracks have been filled with putty and it is oiled or varnished, present a surface of exquisite graining and colour which may be covered in the centre of the room by a large Oriental or home made rug, according to one's means.

Notwithstanding that carpets are breeding places of dust, impurity of air and disease, the other important fact is that they usually use two thirds of the money allotted to furnishing. A really good carpet is thick, closely woven, soft and pliable, with an unobtrusive pattern in rich colours. Wilton and Axminster carpets are the most beautiful carpets in ordinary use and Wilton is the most durable of all carpet materials. Next to it in point of durability is Brussels. A good Brussels always gives satisfaction, but tapestry Brussels does not wear well. In many respects the woman with a rag carpet in her parlour is more to be envied than she who can boast a velvet one. The rag carpet never dictates to the mistress of the house as to the amount of sunlight she may admit while enjoying its company.

Country parlors may be prettily curtained with plain or dotted Swiss muslin, or of scrim edged with antique lace. Nottingham lace, fine in texture and beautiful in finish and design is the most airy and graceful of all curtain materials. The chief object of window hangings is to break up the stiff uniformity of the straight lines of walls and shades and for this purpose even the coarser varieties of Nottingham lace are better than no window drapery at all. Certainly nothing can be in better taste than the rod and rings of our grandparents, which are coming into general use at the present day.

Perhaps her tastes changed as she grew older, or perhaps it was just the simple beauty of the country which she came back to after years in the city, which changed her ideas on decorating. As an eye witness, I can truthfully say that Ethelwyn did NOT have Nottingham lace or any other kind of drapery at her windows at "Tall Evergreens." Roller blinds were installed to keep out the hot summer sun but other than that the windows were bare, to allow the blue of the sky, the green of the trees and the flash of a red winged blackbird as he passed by to enter her domain. When the asparagus patch had turned into a bed of asparagus ferns, Ethelwyn always cut a huge armful of the ferns and brought them into the house to place them in the fireplace. She did not like the empty appearance of the fireplace in the summer time. The ferns brightened up the whole room for a long time.

Although Ethelwyn loved nature and all nature's creatures she had one exception—cats. She didn't really dislike cats as she could always find something good in everything, but she abhorred some of their characteristics. There were always cats around a farm and after observing them for many years she phrased her conclusions in her column in The Globe:

ABOUT CATS

On one occasion Mahomet cut off the skirt of his robe so that he might rise without disturbing the repose of his cat, who was sleeping upon it. Mahomet and I never had much in common and now the last link that bound us is broken. I had turned a chair upside down the moment I discovered our cat asleep upon it. I had told our cat that it might sleep on every other chair in the house except this, and on this chair it should never sleep. It was for THE SIN OF DISOBEDIENCE THAT IT WAS HUSTLED OUT OF EDEN. But I own that a little extra flourish was given to its punishment on account of a sight that I had beheld at early dawn—the sight of an evergreen hedge, with gay little birds skipping from branch to branch, while stealthily stealing along underneath was a deceitful, contemptible, carnivorous brute, that some ladies like to pet.

It is difficult to be indifferent to a cat. One must either hate it or love it and I have no hesitation in enrolling myself among its haters. It seems incapable of conducting itself in a straightforward manner. Instead of being simple and natural it is made up of affectation and sham. Invite it into the house on the coldest night in winter and instead of coming gladly and gratefully forward, it will PRETEND TO HAVE DOUBTS as to the advantages of an indoor life in such a climate. You may say that this is innate modesty; it looks to me like being deceitful above all things. Give a hungry cat a saucer of milk and it will betray no eagerness, no enthusiasm, very little interest. After a few condescending sips it will glance off at vacancy with a discontented air, as though it were meditating "Ah, how much sweeter this milk would taste could I but steal it from a pan with nobody by to see. That is the only way to get the true flavour of milk."

If you want a friend of sweet and caressing manners, who cultivates your acquaintance not because she likes you but because she LIKES YOU TO LIKE HER rest assured that she is a cat. I hate cats.

Let us give the chief of the fallen angels his due and admit that there is some good in cats. They don't get offended easily and they adapt themselves readily to circumstances. Give your dog to understand that you don't want him with you, and what a crestfallen, incredulous, wounded, humiliated, reproachful, miserable look he will give you. Cats don't care so much. I have known a cat to keep right on purring after it had received a direct insult. It may be that the cat's self love is of that tough sort which cannot suffer under a snub, yet I could not but admire the philosophic spirit of our cat yesterday morning, when, after submitting to the law of gravitation, so suddenly brought to bear upon him through the medium of a reversed chair, he quietly went forth to pursue his profession of bird catching, with the air of one to whom nothing particular has happened.

Deaths and funerals were many in the Wetherald family, of course, because it was a large family, but they were more or less looked upon as just as natural a process as birth is. It meant grieving for a time but funerals were something Ethelwyn abhorred.

In an article on death she bared her innermost feelings:

CONCERNING FUNERALS

One of the most dispiriting things in life is the dread of death. There are awful things connected with funerals. Do you think and shudder at the thought of "the crowded, whispering room," the people who come to "pay their last respects" who would a great deal rather stay away and those who have no respects to pay, but a good deal of curiosity to indulge. Anyone who has imagined her own funeral will sincerely wish to spare her relatives and friends the unpleasant duty of attending in person. There is the horrible old aunt who says: "Well she is out of her pain and you have not got the bother of waiting on her now. Good for her, good for you." There are desperate characters who will figure on the cost of the coffin and carriages and others who will desecrate the sanctity of flowers by arranging them in stiff, lifeless masses for ornamental or sentimental purposes. There are idiots who lift up their innocent, tender children, that they may look into the face of Death. There are those who sympathize and don't show it and there are those who don't care much and do show it. There is that unpreventable commingling of the things of time and of those of eternity, which makes the bravest shrink. I think of adding a few clauses to my will which may be called "the last wishes." I notice that the person's last wishes are usually treated with respect and carried out if possible. The first "last wish" will be: Wear no mourning garments.

Colour is a source of consolation not to be despised.

Ethelwyn's talents were many. She could write on almost any imaginable subject with ease and the ability to make it interesting to her readers. Her articles appeared in *New York Independent, New England Magazine, Toronto Week, New York Outlook, Life of New York, Detroit Free Press, Puck, Judge, St. Nicholas* and more.

During a recent research of her work there were over one thousand entries found in regards to both her poetry and prose. She was, indeed, prolific during most of her eighty years, starting at the age of fifteen and continuing until only a few weeks before her death

In 1887 Ethelwyn co-authored a novel with G. Mercer Adams. The book was titled *The Algonquin Maiden*. It might better have been named Ethelwyn's Folly. The book was foreign to her usual style of writing and I am sure she wished that she could have erased the whole experience. This book got poor reviews and was never spoken of at home. I was unaware that it was written until after her death. However, it was reprinted many years later by The Toronto University Press.

.

BACK TO TALL EVERGREENS
✧✧✧

Every large family must have its tragedies and the Wetherald family was no exception. However in Ethelwyn's case the tragedies were interspersed with happy events. It is interesting to note that she was considered the frail one of the family but she lived to nurse her brothers and sisters, to help them through death and to live the longest herself.

In 1888 when Ethelwyn was home for a period of time, she witnessed a family tragedy. The "new" house burned down! By this time the Wetheralds had a large library as books were number one on their list of priorities. One can imagine what panic it was to decide what should be saved first from the fire. The books took precedence. Some must have been lost but in later years there was a large collection of books in the library of the "second new house", some dating back to the 1860s, which proves that they must have been able to save many of them. This would certainly have been in keeping with the Wetherald standards. A book was considered a precious possession. Books were to be treated with respect and never "dog eared". Pages were to be turned with a dry finger, not a finger made moist by a quick trip to the tongue.

At the time of Ethelwyn's death there were several hundred books still in the library. Many of these are now in the Rockwood Academy Collection at University of Guelph and some still are at Tall Evergreens being treasured by Helgi and Kenneth Kernaghan who purchased the farm in 1968.

In 1893 the longing for home, with its smell of apple blossoms and new mown hay, became too strong for Ethelwyn and she came back to the farm, which by now had a name, Tall

Evergreens. The Wetheralds often had visitors from places far enough away that they came by train. When they disembarked at Fenwick station, they invariably had to ask the station agent where the Wetherald farm was. The reply was "go down this road till you come to a long lane of tall evergreen trees - that's the place." So it was only natural that the farm was known from then on as Tall Evergreens.

Back home again Ethelwyn was inspired by nature wherever she looked. Verse started to pour out and onto paper. Her poetry at this time was filled with thoughts on nature—rain, wind and the seasons—as if she had rediscovered the wonder of country living after having lived so long in the city where her work and interests had taken her.

She had a mysterious manner of describing Nature as displayed in the following poem:

THE SHY SUN

The sun went with me to the wood,
    And lingered at the door;
One glance he gave from where he stood
    But dared not venture more;

Nor knew that in the heart of her
    Who felt his presence nigh,
His love was all the lovelier
    Because his look was shy.

She had love for all facets of nature and delighted in putting her feelings in rhyme in a sweet, abstract manner. She was once spoken of in a news story as "the priestess of trees, flowers, wind and rain". So in tune with rhythm was she, that it is hard to believe that Ethelwyn could not hold a tune. She loved music and would often start to sing and all was well for the first few bars but then abruptly she was off key. However she wrote several poems which were put to music, even as late as 1981 when her "The Wise Frog" was set to music by Ruth Watson Henderson, while Keith Bissell set her "April" and "The Ploughman" to music in 1958 and 1959 respectively many years after her death. "Dead Leaves" had been put to music many years before. In all, seven of her poems became songs.

In many of her poems Ethelwyn describes her own life style and her communion with Nature.

A RAINY MORNING

The low sky, and the warm, wet wind,
    And the tender light on the eyes;
A day like a soul that has never sinned,
    New dropped from Paradise.

And 'tis oh, for a long walk in the rain,
    By the side of the warm, wet breeze,
With the thoughts washed clean of dust and stain
    As the leaves on the shining trees.

Even though she had meant to stay home when she came back to Tall Evergreens in 1893, she could not turn down an invitation she received in 1895. It was to fill a position as assistant to Francis Bellamy, editor of *The Ladies Home Journal*. So she took off once more for Philadelphia.

However, after the solitude and slow pace of country living she stated that:

"My work was altogether critical—the reading of manuscripts which came in by the hundred every day and writing out an estimate of worthwhile articles of their availability for the Journal. In some ways I enjoyed the experience, but it was a lasting dissatisfaction to feel, at the end of each day, that I was too tired to do any creative work of my own."

It was in this era that she also worked as assistant to Forrest Morgan, the editor of *The World's Best Literature*, where she got eighteen dollars a week— a really high rate of pay for those days. When that work was finished she was offered a position as first class proof reader at an even larger salary but she longed for home. This time she summed up her feeling:

"There was an indefinable feeling that too much 'learned lumber in the head' must crush out whatever repressed spontaneous growth of my own was still surviving."

So she took off once more for the solitude of Tall Evergreens, this time to stay. Her poem says it all:

THE OLD HOME

My thoughts are with my far home, my old home, my
 only home,
 My mother waiting at the door to welcome me within;
Her eyes are like November leaves upon the furrowed,
 lonely loam,
 Her hair is white as night-frost when all the boughs
 are thin.

I want to see the moon climb the arms of our great pine
 again,
 I want to feel the dew fall upon the pasture path,
I want to haunt the wood glades and dream that they are
 mine again,
 I want to hear the Bob White across the aftermath.

I want to see the white stream in springtime burst its tomb
 again,

> I want to feel the young grass about my jaded feet,
> I want to set my heart free and give it air and room
> again
> To move to those forgotten strains to which it used to
> beat.
>
> Oh mother, mother, mother, do you know that barefoot
> boy of yours,
> Who went up to the city and was lost in heat and strife,
> Has found no bliss that matches with that quiet harvest joy
> of yours?
> That wealth and depth of living beggars all that he
> called life.
>
> My thoughts are with my old home, my wide-boughed,
> clover-meadowed home,
> Astir beneath the skies of peace when morning birds
> begin,
> Asleep beneath the early stars , my deep-grassed ivy-
> shadowed home,
> With Mother waiting at the door to welcome me within.

By 1895 she had amassed quite a collection of poems so had her first book of poetry published. The title was *The House of the Trees and Other Poems.*

By now Ethelwyn's family was pretty well strewn around the continent. Her favourite brothers Sam and Fred were in St. Paul, Minnesota with Great Northern Railway, Charlie was in California and Jane in Edmonton. Jim had died and Lewis ran away from home at a very early age never to be heard of again. Herbert and William Jr. were left on the farm along with their mother Jemima and father William. Ethelwyn made a fifth when she came home.

In 1898 William Sr. who had been in failing health,

decided to take a trip to England to see all his old relatives and friends once more. While there he contracted pneumonia and died. He was buried at Banbury. His death must have been a great loss as one gets the feeling that he was the hub of the Wetherald family wheel. Now the family on the farm was down to Ethelwyn, her mother and two brothers, William and Herbert.

One wonders if her father's death had anything to do with her poem:

THE PLOUGHMAN

I heard the ploughman sing in the wind,
    And sing right merrily,
As down in the cold of the sunless mould
    The grasses buried he.

And now the grasses sing in the wind,
    Merrily do they sing,
While down in the cold of the sunless mold
    Is the ploughman slumbering.

Ethelwyn had a great sense of humour and occasionally it broke out on paper. She could laugh with the world or laugh at herself which is a great trait to have.

IF YOU WORRY

You're either feeble mentally
Or else defective dentally
Or your liver and your nerves have
    ceased to rhyme.

You may have pangs rheumatic
Or else up in your attic.
Is the picture of some ancestor
Who worried all the time.
The trouble may be nutritive,
Or else upon a toot-rative,
You go alas too frequently with consequent regret.
You exercise rambunctiously,
Or else you gobble unctuously,
When gastronomic pleasures are upon the table set.
And so you keep on worrying and flurrying and hurrying
From specialist to specialist until you're like to flop;
Just take some good advice from me
I will not look or listen - see?
But I just everlastingly STOP!

The following anecdote, was inspired by her younger brother:

JACK'S GRACE

"Jack" said the young mother "what is the reason you have to be told over and over again and over and over again and over and over again:

Say your grace before you start to eat."

Jack put down his spoon, folded his hands and prayed:

"Oh God our Father in Heaven, what is ze reason you have to be told over and over again and over and over again and over and over again —Bless zis food and make me a good boy Amen."

Another example of her readiness to laugh at herself is implanted in my memory. She had been a friend of Louis Blake Duff (then editor of Welland Tribune) for quite some time but only through correspondence. She had never met him face to face or even seen a picture of him. One Christmas she felt that she would like to present him with a little gift to show her appreciation of his friendship. She carefully chose a comb and brush set, wrapped it up and sent it. In due time she received a note thanking her for such "an appropriate gift". A few weeks later Ethelwyn was reading the newspaper when she suddenly burst out laughing. When I went to her to see what was so hilarious she said to me:

"Look at this picture and the name under it!".

I looked and there was a picture of Louis Blake Duff with his shiny bald head—not a hair on it! She took it all in good nature and decided to check things out in the future if she was about to give a gift.

She had a burning desire to live for one hundred years but she knew that it was very unlikely. However as long as she was on this earth she wanted to retain some youth, not just in appearance, but in her style of thinking.

SOUL AND BODY

The body says: 'I am thirsty,'
    The body says: 'I am cold,'
The body says: 'I am weary,'
    And last of all: 'I am old.'

And for its thirst there is water
    And shelter and warmth in the blast
And for its ache there is slumber
    But it dies, it dies at last.

> But I am a soul, please Heaven
>> And though I freeze in my cage,
> Or burn in a sleepless fever,
>> I shall live untouched of age.

In 1904 Ethelwyn's book *The Radiant Road* was published and in 1907 *The Last Robin* came out. By the time this book was published Ethelwyn had accumulated an abundance of poems which she had written over the years—most of them sold.

In 1908 Ethelwyn lost her mother. Death was taking its toll on the Wetherald family. With her mother gone she had to shoulder the whole burden of the household work, which did not leave her much time to display her talents.

❖❖❖

Ethelwyn in Her Youth

Tall Evergreens in the early 1900s

THE HOUSE IN THE TREES
✧✧✧

Ethelwyn's favourite brother Sam was making a visit to the old homestead when a new idea came up which eventually made its way into literary history. He built a tree house for her. She wrote many poems in this tree house and it became a part of her life. Later on she wrote a sketch of how it all came about, leaving the history of her very own house in a tree where she must have had many inspirations for her writing.

The story in Ethelwyn's own words will be much better than mine even though I remember the house well and slept in it with her many times. Snuggled down under a blanket we could peek out to see the moonbeams reflecting in the nearby pond. A friendly owl hooted once in a while and the breeze rustling through the branches was our lullaby for sleep.

People from miles around used to visit Tall Evrgreens and ask to go up into her House in the Trees. The neighbour boy she refers to in her story was Duncan Armbrust, who lived on Poth St. and loved to visit Ethelwyn.

> It was the neighbour's boy who began it. One hot summer evening, when he was over here, he happened to remark that in their back yard was a spreading apple tree and in that apple tree he had made a platform, to which on a warm night one could convey a pallet of straw, a blanket and a pillow, and sleep out among the leaves, the tree toads and the stars. Instantly the iron of envy entered my soul, and has only recently been extracted by the Visiting Brother. "Why not have a house in a tree?" said he.

"In what tree?" was the breathless counter-inquiry. "There are plenty of trees big enough and strong enough to support a few boards with a cot-bed thereon, but–"

"But," he continued, "a real little house with walls and floor and roof and a front door that could be locked might be built in our old willow."

We rushed down the new-moon-shaped path to the willow, which is a giant among its kind, stretching out its limbs to the pond on the west, to the asparagus bed, the Sweet Bough and Snow apple trees on the south.

"I suppose a house under a tree wouldn't do" said the Visiting Brother, in that teasing way he has.

"Oh, the idea! Under a tree! Anyone could have a house under a tree. No, it's in a tree that I want it, with the fresh air and the leaves blowing all around it and under it, and the birds flying in and out, and not a vestige of dampness anywhere. Couldn't it be ten feet above the ground?"

"Yes it would have to be at least that," said the Visiting Brother. "It might be six by eight," he continued, casting a calculating glance into the branches.

"Oh, yes, do have it six by eight"

The work began forthwith. Happily, there were boards left over from the straw-shed built near the barn, but it was necessary to bring poles from the woods, and to procure spikes, nails, hinges, and screws from the store. Hatchet and hammer rang merrily out on the pleasant March air and in a week it was finished----all but the mosquito netting and the awnings. The way into my parlour is up not a winding stair, but a ladder. An ash pole with the bark on serves as a bannister. At the top of the ladder is a landing, and just in front is a rustic out-of-door seat, set in among the greening and yellowing willow shoots. On the left is the door of the mansion, which, when opened discloses two articles of furniture. One is a broad seat running the length of the house, and which is designed

"A double debt to pay; A bed by night, a davenport by day."

The other piece of furniture is a small table. Mattress cushions and a steamer rug embellish the seat, while the table is fitted out with books and pencils, paper and ink. The entire edifice is braced and supported by the southward-stretching limbs of the willow, yet it doesn't present an unbalanced appearance as there are a number of unweighted limbs. Seen from the side road, the house in the willow might be mistaken for a huge unfinished dry goods box, did not the steeply sloping roof with its unmistakable eaves and charming air of crowning a worthy achievement show to all the world around that it is a real house—meant to work in, rest in, sleep in.

On the night of the 5th of March the builder slept in it, with a cool breeze just at freezing flowing through (for there is nearly as much window space as wall space), and no disturbance save an occasional inquisitive squirrel and the softly gurgling brook.

"In the wide awe and wonder of the night," what dreams may not have come to him, what secrets may not have been revealed? Purity and loneliness, and the brook-song in the ears, and on all sides the wise old willow busily perfecting her buds. We are a part of nature. What buds of promise might not be perfected in us if we were nearer to the skyey influence!

By day it is a cheery spot. The sun shines so warmly at the south it might almost be called a solarium and when Sol is behind a cloud it is as least an airium. We have half a dozen names for it: "The Air Castle". "The Eyrie", The Bird's Nest", "The Retreat", "The Dream of Summer", and another very charming little name made of the initials of all the ten different woods that go into its construction. There is pine in the floor and roof, hemlock in the joists, elm, linden and birch in the seat, ironwood and cherry in the railings outside, ash and maple in the door posts and spruce in the siding. It's a very woodsy house.

But its chief beauty lies in the fact that it is in a tree. The summer house built on the ground, under a group of evergreens, is dank, not to say soggy and open to the "varmints and serpentine insects" that may stroll up from the pond, whereas "The Eyrie" is dried out with sun and wind within a hour after a spring rain. Another great attraction is the fact that the tree in which it finds shelter is a willow. As I write these words the whistles are ripening on all sides of me and above my table.

Although the above seems to tell us that the house was called The Eyrie and may have been temporarily, the permanent name was Camp Shelbi which was spelled out in pine cones nailed up on one wall. It was this name that spelled out the ten woods that were used in its construction.

I believe that it was built in 1911 and withstood many a fierce storm without becoming loosened from the limbs it was built on. Its strength outlived that of the tree it was built in and in 1921 a particularly vicious storm broke off the main branch on which it was located. That was the end of Ethelwyn's House in The Trees.

Camp Shelbi - Ethelwyn Wetherald second from left

ETHELWYN THE MOTHER
❖❖❖

It was 1911, and Ethelwyn was fifty-four, when a "miracle" happened which would make a profound difference in the lives of three people. It was apple picking and packing time which meant that there were extra farm hands to feed. Ethelwyn advertised for help since the housework had become too much for her alone. A young woman, separated from her husband, with a five month old baby applied for the job. Ethelwyn had not bargained for a baby but the mother seemed very capable so she gave it a try. Mary and the baby moved in and soon were a part of the family.

Ethelwyn soon found that the baby had become the most important part of her life. Two years later when the mother decided to move back to the big city, where she would have more social life than was offered in the country, Ethelwyn persuaded her to leave the baby "on the farm where she will be healthier and you may come back any time you wish." This was agreed upon.

Ethelwyn's Baby

A year later Ethelwyn, who was beginning to feel that her world would collapse should the baby be taken from her, again used her powers of persuasion in order to adopt the baby. Mary knew that her child would have a future and security in the Wetherald home and made the right decision. Ethelwyn was most understanding and thoughtful about the adoption, agreeing to have the baby's mother visit any time she wished for as long as she wished. Ethelwyn once said she would never have been able to live with herself had she barred a mother from her child. But she did give the baby a new name—Dorothy. This name she explained later meant "gift of God". From then on Mary was always Mama and Ethelwyn was Nan. As time went by there was no doubt in Dorothy's mind as to which place was "home"—Mama's in the city or Nan's on the farm.

Ethelwyn loved children but never married to have her own. The midwife present at her birth, who was no doubt misinformed, later told her that she should never marry as she was too slender to bear children. Unfortunately Ethelwyn took this advice seriously. She had a romance, some details of which she once told me but when the subject of children was raised, the man in her life revealed that having children was very important to him and so the romance died. However they remained friends and valued each other's opinions in the world of literature. Ironically, he later married another woman who never had any children.

Ethelwyn now had something precious in her life and it sparked her sixth book of poems, this time children's poems, *Tree Top Mornings*, published in 1921. She dedicated this book to her daughter Dorothy. The dedication was a very short, true story of love between mother and child which indicated that Dorothy was truly her own. It was a simple little story of an incident which had really happened. It read:

TO DOROTHY

One bright morning a year ago, when I said goodbye in a Run-along-now- as-I-am -very-busy tone of voice, you turned to me with tears, exclaiming: "When you send me off to school without one happy word it makes my feelings feel bad!" And so Dorothy–My Little Heart– I am inscribing all these happy words to you in the hope that they will make your feelings feel good.

My Adopted Daughter

My small adopted daughter
   Is four years old today,
Her rosy face is round and fair,
   Her eyes are bluish gray.
Above them hangs her hair, as thick
   And sweet as meadow hay.

Her dimpled hands are quick and strong,
Her eager feet are light,
I think of her the whole day long,
I hear her breathe at night,

She makes me doubly hate the wrong,
And doubly love the right.

> She comes to me for warmth
>   and bread,
> For help and comradeship.
> Hides on my breast her
>   drooping head,
> Her tears and grieving lip;
> And all my heart is comforted
>   Beneath her sorrow's grip.
>
> "And people say, 'How fortunate
>   This child! Of that we're sure.
> Such friends, such prospects,
>   such a home
> For her, adrift and poor.
> 'Tis to be hoped her gratitude
>   So active – will endure.'"
>
> Ah, little child, they do not see
>   The food I take from you:
> The flower like love, the purity
>   As clean as morning dew,
> The April youthfulness that makes
>   My task of living new.

Her love for her child seemed to shine out of everything she wrote, as in the above hand-written poem found among her keepsakes after her death.

Ethelwyn had an uncanny understanding of children and a most unusual way of handling the problems which, as any mother knows, comes with children.

When I was around twelve I let Ethelwyn know that I definitely wanted to be a "chorus girl", having undoubtedly seen a vaudeville show and been fascinated with the dancers. The thought of her "baby" becoming a chorus girl must have been shocking to a gentle Quaker minister's daughter, but she handled it in her understanding manner. Not wanting to destroy her daughter's initiative by flatly refusing, she simply answered: "That might be all right, but you are a little young yet. Wait until you are fifteen and we will go to New York together and you can see if you would like it."

Three years seemed like an eternity but we sealed the bargain and I settled down to wait for my entrance into the bright lights of Broadway. Of course by the time the three years had passed Ethelwyn's problem had vanished. I had completely forgotten my childish whim and was off in another direction. She simply could not hurt a child's feelings and she was uncannily wise in her ways of getting around problems without hurting or destroying a child's confidence.

Her insight into human nature was woven into her simple stories of everyday life. In one of her later stories she tells the tale of an event when her two uncles (John and Thomas) in their youth had been severely whipped for some infraction. Along with this story she sums up her own views on the effect of punishment in general:

> And was the will of either Uncle John or Uncle Thomas really broken? If so it wasn't noticeable. Honest, upright, kindly and determined men, they gave the impression that no one's will can be broken, except by consent of the owner of that will. Flesh and feelings may be hurt but in the cool citadel of the soul, where Justice reigns, there is, by every severe punishment, a strengthening of the moral fibre.

When there was need for her to punish me, she never resorted to slapping or spanking. Her form of punishment was to go to the clock and point to a time which was a half hour or an hour hence. Then she put her fingers to her lips. This meant that she would not speak to me for a half hour or hour.

To me this was absolutely the worst form of punishment, since what child does not have something to say or exclaim about or question every few minutes. Being cut off from my most loved person in the world was a lesson not to be quickly forgotten.

One time, Uncle Herbert, incensed over something I had done that was pretty bad, insisted that I needed a good spanking. To appease him Ethelwyn agreed and took me into another room. Here she admonished me for what I had done and said that she had to spank me because she had given her word to her brother that she would. "But" she told me, "you holler when I give you the first spank. Holler good and loud." She put me over her knee and when she gently slapped my bottom I hollered—good and loud as I had been told. Uncle Herbert, hearing the screams, took for granted that I had been duly punished, Ethelwyn had come out of the situation with a clear conscience, and I had not been hurt.

She did not push religion upon me, but often talked of various beliefs and gave me thoughts to ponder on as I grew older. We went to church by way of horse and buggy. It was three miles to the Friends Church. She always encouraged me to take part in the Christmas concerts which I enjoyed. Sometimes we read from the bible after a Sunday dinner, each taking a turn, but other than that, Ethelwyn believed in letting me form my own opinions and create my own religious beliefs.

She was always a good hostess to cousins from Rockwood, when they came to the Friends Church Quarterly or Yearly Meetings in Pelham. They attended the meeting and then walked the three miles to Tall Evergreens where they usually stayed all night and discussed family news and happenings at Rockwood.

When her book *Tree Top Mornings* came out in 1921 her mood was one of happiness as is expressed in the following poem:

A LOVELY TIME

When I was a girl in youth's fair clime
All my thought was a 'lovely time'
A perfectly lovely time indeed
Was the length and the depth and the height
    of my need.
I said, I will work and think and plan
To have just as good a time as I can;
And life shall be, when I come to my prime,
That grand, sweet song called 'A Lovely Time'.

Well now with my love for my brothers four,
My sisters and parents and neighbours, a score,
My friends who number a hundred and three,
And my own adorable family,
My love for my baby, my love for my home
My love for all lovers wherever they roam,
My busy life, like a silver chime,
Is a lovely tune to a Lovely Time.

Anyone who is predisposed to writing verse knows what havoc interruption can cause, when the lines have all but been established in one's mind, but not yet down on paper. Ethelwyn must have gone through this experience hundreds of times with a small child around to ask a myriad of questions but she always had time to pause and answer with no impatience whatsoever.

Although she undoubtedly would rather have had her pen in hand, she always took time to comfort her child. In one of her columns in *The Star Weekly* she bared her feelings when she wrote:

"Every modern woman hates her apron—until her child dries her tears on it."

One of her poems clearly states her priorities:.

AS GOOD AS A THRONE

Here is a thought as good as a throne
 I am my own, yes wholly my own,
No burdensome parent and nobody's wife
 I can simply do as I choose with my life!
True I have millions of human brothers,
 But they have no claim on me at all,
I certainly shall not live for others
 Nor hear an imagined duty's call.

So I stretched out my feet, as women will,
 To the open fire, for the day was chill;
When, swift as the rush of running water
 Burst in my little adopted daughter.

She wanted ice cream—the half of a brick
 She wanted help in arithmetic
She wanted to know the reason why
 I had not made a blueberry pie.
She wanted sympathy, candy and ink,
 She wanted a dress of rosy pink,
And help in collecting leaves and barks –

At this, with a few sarcastic remarks,
 My Ownness arose and wished me 'Good Day!'
And all in reply that I could say
 Was, 'Thrones are no good anyway!'

WHO WAS ETHELWYN?
✧✧✧

Ethelwyn enjoyed travel and the company of friends although she was a very retiring person later in life. One of her most valued memories was that of a trip to the Thousand Islands where her friend Helena Coleman had a cottage on an Island named "Pinehurst". She was one of several lady guests including Marjorie Pickthall and a guest from Australia. She always carried memories of the St. Lawrence river gushing by their door and of early morning talks and walks and five o'clock tea—an occasional trip to the mainland by canoe to purchase groceries and on Sunday taking the maid to church via boat. While the maid sat in church, Ethelwyn and her hostess waited in the boat, enjoying the opportunity to observe nature on Lake Ontario's shore.

Pinehurst- Island home of Helena Coleman

As I write this story of Ethelwyn I ponder on who she really was. Was she the woman of the 1880s and 90s who was filled with confidence in her writing? The columnist who wrote articles in the largest newspaper in Canada on subjects such as decorating a house, as would a professional decorator. A person who did not have her parlour decorated in the manner in which she had advised other people. Or was she as I knew her, a quiet, unassuming person, who filled reams of paper with her writing but who very seldom left the farm to visit? A person who seemed anything but worldly, but who actually had done more traveling than most other women of that time. A person who in her teens, at her father's bidding, took on the responsibility of learning how to run a printing press alongside all men in the office of *The Tribune*, while in later life she admitted hating anything mechanical and also to being "a moron" when it came to mathematics. A woman who put all else aside to care for her adopted daughter. As I look back, the Ethelwyn I knew and the author Ethelwyn I write about now are two different individuals.

She had been brought up in an extremely religious atmosphere, where silent blessing was observed before every meal and a few verses from the bible were read after the meal. Silent blessing was a period of perhaps one minute, when everyone at the table bowed his head and talked to God privately. It was no doubt more beneficial to the soul, as one could say things to God silently that might not have been voiced aloud. Ethelwyn, no doubt, went to church for many years of her life but during my time with her she went only occasionally. It was a three mile trip by horse and buggy.

She had a fairly strict code. One's word must be kept at all costs. A Quaker and especially a Wetherald must always honour a promise. She drew a strong line between right and wrong, truth and falsehoods, arrogance and humility. She detested swearing and dirty words but once stated that if she had to use one or the other she would use the swear word rather than a dirty word.

She did have great faith in the hereafter and approached religion in an intelligent manner. She theorized that if a power (God) created us, then He must have a place for us in Eternity. He surely would not destroy his own creations. There had to be a reason for existence and life here was only a step in our spiritual evolution. She never intimated that we would go either to Heaven or Hell, and I am sure she did not believe that we must go to one place or the other. She simply believed that there is another chapter in the book of life, which we cannot comprehend until we reach and turn the final page.

Ethelwyn was an extremely well-informed person in both politics and world affairs, and it is very doubtful that she would find it hard to discuss any subject one might broach. Having received a large part of her education in United States, it was only natural that she would be as interested in their politics as well as those of Canada. She always subscribed to a Toronto newspaper as well as a local paper as she felt that one must know what is going on in the whole world to be properly informed. Of course the Toronto paper arrived at our country mail box a day after it was printed, but that made no difference in the slow pace of life at that time. She was also very adept at quotes. Just ask her to match a quote with the name of the author and she could answer instantaneously.

Ethelwyn was a very meticulous person and most particular about personal grooming. She worked hard in the house all morning, perhaps washing or ironing with the old flat irons which had to be heated on the top of the wood burning stove, but as soon as the mid-day meal was over and all dishes washed, she always disappeared up to her bedroom where she had her daily bath and changed to fresh clothes, combed and brushed her hair, then reappeared downstairs as fresh as a daisy. One of her favourite sayings was: "Cleanliness is next to Godliness".

She also traveled extensively in her younger years with her favourite brother Sam, to Florida and various other parts of the United States. When Sam and Fred took up residence in Minnesota, she traveled to that state to visit them. Although remembered as a person frail in stature, she had been an ardent horseback rider in younger years. While in London, Ontario, she took lessons in horseback riding which came in good stead a little later on when she visited relatives on their ranch in Iowa. Here she often went on 20 mile rides in the moonlight and stated that "no mere motor car could give me such pleasure as that."

And again I wonder—who was Ethelwyn Wetherald? Was she the robust horseback rider or the gentle lady I knew who enjoyed nothing more than a quiet afternoon with her pen, a filled ink-well and reams of paper? In a house, which in those days was not filled with obnoxious noise from a radio or television, a person in the next room could plainly hear her pen scratching her thoughts onto paper as she wrote.

It is quite interesting to look at her thoughts on health. In 1937 when she was 80 years old she wrote this witty but informative essay:

> Ninety nine times out of 100 the human body breaks down (at the age of 50, 60 or 70) but if it lasts till 80 or 90 it is a safe guess that it is wearing out. There is always somewhere a weakest spot and a chain is no stronger than its defective link.
>
> If your lungs are especially strong, your kidneys may be weak. If you can eat any old thing and don't know you have a stomach you'll soon find out you have chronic catarrh or catch cold easily; if you are proud of your splendid muscles you will probably die after an "attack" from that usually meek and gentle creature, the human heart. "Beware the anger of a patient man" is especially true of the heart.
>
> Up to a certain age it will cheerfully allow you any number of break neck stunts but it draws the line and as an attacker it never says your money or your life. What it bags is your life.
>
> Of the liver, we hear more evil reports than of all the other organs put together. Like Dicken's Fat Boy its chief occupation in life is snoozing .The sluggish liver never attacks anyone. Its specialty is life long persecution in which it is ably assisted by its twin brother Dyspepsia.. Battle, murder and sudden death are angels of mercy compared with these twin demons. The man they claim for their own is

almost absolutely sure to be a centenarian. Though it may be said of him that "he died of a Sunday" it is doubtful that he will die of anything else.

Even mental weaknesses affect the health. Here is an individual apparently in perfect condition, skin, lungs, stomach, kidneys, liver, bowels, sight, hearing, muscles, all in ideal health. As an infant he captured first prize at all the baby shows, but as he grows into manhood you notice he avoids people, prefers his own company to that of anyone else, is inclined to be self sufficient, scowls at the radio and ignores the telephone. The weakest spot is in the nerves. He will have a nervous breakdown, spend weeks or months in "The City of Dreadful Night". A frequent disease of the nerves is worry. Every wife of an easy going husband takes it out on her nerves when she tearfully exclaims: "Someone has got to do the worrying."

Without arguing the point it has been suggested that the wisest plan is to worry just enough to keep out of the poor house and not enough to land one in an insane asylum. Disease by any name means lack of ease. Our pioneer forefathers who lived for months on salt pork and buckwheat cakes, suffered from the itch; we call it eczema. They ground through fever and ague while we "run a temperature". Never having heard of vitamins they knew what scurvy meant. When the high blood pressure reached its highest altitude it was known as a "stroke." Disease may have a thousand names, a hundred characteristics, but its nature is invariably the absence of ease. Although happiness is our being's end aim, it is a shy bird, difficult to capture and ease is a pretty satisfactory substitute.

TRAGEDIES
✧✧✧

In 1918 Ethelwyn's brother, Will left home driving the horse hooked to the buggy to make a visit to Welland. He took a neighbour with him. It was always considered an hour drive there, an hour to return and a couple of hours to spend doing whatever business they went for. So when mid-afternoon arrived Ethelwyn started looking for them to return. What she saw was shocking. The neighbour was coming up the lane leading the horse—no buggy–no Will. Soon she was told that her brother was in hospital from injuries from an accident in town—the buggy was demolished. A few days later Will came home but succumbed to his injuries and died on August 8, 1918.

One might think that a person who poured out such beautiful verse as Ethelwyn did would not be able or willing to take on manual work. Far be it! Now that brother Herbert was the only man on the farm, she knew that he would need help. She was often to be seen driving a team of horses pulling a spray wagon, while Herbert walked alongside wielding the long wand which spewed out the spray onto the trees in the orchards. During hay time she went out in the field on scorching hot days to help Herbert bring in the hay.

As he pitched the hay onto the wagon she "tramped it down", keeping it spread evenly over the wagon so that the load would be stable to drive in to the barn. Other lighter chores, such as feeding chickens, gathering eggs, or carrying a pail of water to a thirsty cow tethered far from water, were also taken care of by her, but there is no doubt that while she was performing these chores, there were verses forming in her mind about something she was observing as the following poem implies:

APPLE BLOSSOMS

Amid the young year's breathing hopes,
    When eager grasses wrap the earth
I see on greening orchard slopes
    The blossoms trembling into birth.
They open wide their rosy palms
    To feel the hesitating rain,
Or beg a longed-for golden alms
    From skies that deep in clouds have lain.

They mingle with the bluebird's songs,
    And with the warm wind's reverie;
To sward and stream their snow belongs,
    To neighbouring pines in flocks they flee.
O doubly crowned with breathing hopes
    The branches bending down to earth
That feel on greening orchard slopes
    Their blossoms trembling into birth!

    Small household chores were plenteous in those days, the least of which was caring for the lamps. Every day the coal oil lamps had to have the glass "chimney" cleaned, the wick trimmed and the lamp filled with oil. As soon as it was too dark to see in the evening, they were lit. Lifting the glass chimney off, a lit match was touched to the wick which had the other end down in the oil, the chimney was put back on again and the wick adjusted to just the right height to give the best light without any flicker. It was a very yellow light but it seemed to be sufficient for the reading Ethelwyn did. Many an evening Uncle Herbert and I listened as Ethelwyn read to us out of *The Saturday Evening Post* holding the magazine close to the flickering light. That way we could all enjoy the story together.

All the water for the house had to be pumped up from the outdoor well a few yards from the back door. Cooking was done on a wood burning stove and the weekly washing was done in a hand-rocked washer. Ethelwyn always arose at 6:30 every morning to start a new fire, as it was allowed to go out each night. There was no other heat in the house. Neither was there electricity in the house, nor radio, television or telephone. Transportation was by foot or horse and buggy. A walk of two miles to the nearest village of Fenwick or the little grocery store at Chantler was made frequently. Any destination further than this necessitated hitching up the horse and buggy for the journey. A trip to Welland with horse and buggy was close to an all day excursion. Farm life could be a very lonely life but it suited Ethelwyn's personality perfectly. Occasionally she rode the train from Fenwick or Chantler station to Hamilton or Toronto to shop or visit friends.

She had the burden of nursing her sister Jane in 1922, when Jane came home from Edmonton very ill and died a few months later. Several times she also nursed her favourite brother, Sam, back to health from a nervous breakdown. He came home from St. Paul and at one time was on the farm with her for several years recuperating. He was so sensitive that the clocks in the house had to be stopped because the ticking drove him to distraction and we had to speak in whispers. When nursing her nerve-stricken brother she gave him complete assurance, complied with his every wish, agreed with his every thought, while denying her own feelings. She had to think up ways to keep her youngster happy because playmates on the premises were too much for Sam. But her patience never wavered and she gave in to every whim Sam had, while at the same time devising ways to make life happy for her daughter. In 1927 Sam came back to the farm to die. By now Ethelwyn was seventy and was becoming somewhat frail, but despite this she faithfully nursed her brother, getting up in the middle of the night to turn him from side to side for weeks until the end came. Although still a child at this time, I could sense the sorrow she was experiencing. But there were no tears. She firmly believed that tears are shed because one is feeling sorry for oneself and that is selfish.

Ethelwyn inherited all of Sam's savings. The smell of money must have reached a few investment salesmen, for they lost no time in finding her. Stock in bogus gas wells, loans to neighbours and gifts to relatives and friends soon depleted her entire bank account. Still she did not complain. Fortune did not look kindly upon her efforts to write, for times had changed. Of course, she was not alone, for this was during the Great Depression and everyone was suffering from the same disease—poverty. A tiny person in later years, perhaps a hundred pounds, she still had a spirit as strong as her body was frail. She was a veritable mountain of strength to those around her, never giving up hope when things were adverse, accepting the inevitable with dignity, complete resignation and faith.

With her sense of humour she had a unique manner in handling would-be borrowers. Knowing how hard-up a farmer can be at certain times of the year, she could not bring herself to refuse a loan—which she never seemed to get back—much less with interest. After a few of these episodes she realized that this could not go on indefinitely, so devised a plan "which should put a stop to it" she said. When someone asked for a $100.00 loan, she would sweetly reply that she simply could not make a mere loan to such a good friend or neighbout but would "rather present you with an outright gift of half the amount---$50.00." Her debtors must have been dazed by this offer but no doubt took her up on it.

"But" she reasoned, "what person could possibly come back to me and ask for another loan after that? Besides, it is easier to part with $50.00 as a gift than to part with $100.00 as a loan, which I'll never get back anyway." All this in face of the fact that she was running low on money, her poetry was not selling as it always had and the farm was not producing more than enough to pay the taxes.

In 1931 with six published books of poetry behind her, the last book— *Lyrics and Sonnets* came off the press. But the glow of the new book was soon gone when the following year she lost her brother Herbert. This meant hiring help on the farm In the early 1930s when electricity was brought to the farm, it meant that the house had lights in every room and it was no longer necessary to use coal oil lamps. However, Ethelwyn could not bring herself to simply push a mysterious button on the wall to turn on the upstairs lights when going to bed. She still carried a lamp for a long time after the system was installed. When one has performed a task in a certain manner for seventy-five years, it is too hard to change and I think she always had the feeling that if she pushed the switch for lights, something unexpected might happen with which she would be unable to cope. However, in time she did cast aside the old way for the new.

In 1936 Ethelwyn fell and broke a hip. Again she proved that her spirit was as strong as her body was frail. In those days hip replacements were unknown. The usual treatment was to put weights on the leg to keep it from being shorter and then let Nature take her course in healing. But this was very painful. Fortunately her doctor was an understanding country doctor and did not want to put her through the pain so he let her heal without them. When she was walking again she had to have a special shoe with a built-up sole to even out the length of her legs. Even while she was in bed she just kept on writing down verse as it came to her. Eventually she was able to walk and rejoiced at being able to once again sit at her oval writing table which she had used for many years, nestled close to a sunny south window. Here she wrote her poetry and kept up her correspondence with friends far and wide.

Her correspondence was a major factor in her life as she could communicate with her friends without having to go anywhere. She wrote to many people whom she had never met but always felt that she knew them intimately—and she no doubt did. Ethelwyn had many famous friends and correspondents—Marjorie Pickthall, Helena Coleman, Wilson Macdonald, Wallace Havelock Robb, Walter McRaye, Bliss Carmen, John Garvin, G. D. Roberts and Earl Grey. She had an autographed painting by Paul Peel, also a friend.

By now things had changed in the world of poetry and she found that markets for her poetic style were few and far between. So she concentrated on writing stories of her family and her childhood at Rockwood, parts of which are in this book. She knew many people "on paper" but was not a person to visit in her later years. Living in the country on a farm which was two miles from the nearest village, walking was the usual method of transportation and this probably influenced her decision to stay at home. What more likely caused her to withdraw was the fact that she had become very deaf, which could have been too embarrassing for her to cope with in groups. However, she loved her correspondents who were many and scattered in different countries.

Ethelwyn's strong sense of caring for others was demonstrated in the 1930s when she took a neighbour's child into her home and provided him with schooling even though at that time she was very low in money. When the neighbour child, during a conversation with Ethelwyn, had stated that he wanted to go to high school but couldn't because of family troubles she immediately offered him assistance—a place to live in her house and books for school. (Students had to buy all their own books in those days.) Perhaps she was recalling her own youth and somehow repaying the old favour received when a family friend in Buffalo furnished Ethelwyn with several years of education in the United States.

In the late 1930s, just to keep her hand in, Ethelwyn

started to contribute to a column in the *Welland Tribune.* It was a children's column written by Mrs. S. McInnis, under the pen name of Patty Perkins, who was thrilled to have Ethelwyn as a contributor. Ethelwyn wanted to stay in the background so used the penname "Octo" since she was now an octogenarian. She enjoyed her new "job" and answered every letter the children wrote to her. I am sure she now felt that she had come alive again. It had been many years since she last wrote in a newspaper column and even though she was now writing for a very small newspaper, it gave her the wonderful opportunity to live once again in a writers' world where she belonged. She was making children happy as well as helping Patty Perkins who delighted in the arrangement. The children all came to love Octo and wrote her many letters, some asking questions about the "long ago" and some confiding their dreams and worries which every child has. Eventually Patty Perkins launched the news of who Octo really was.

But it was still the Dirty Thirties and Ethelwyn was feeling the pinch along with everyone else. However, she was not worried about having money to spend on herself. Her essay below tells just how she felt about it.

GIVING TO THE POOR

Although I seldom mention it, as I dislike to discuss monetary matters and invite invidious comparison, I am really in pretty comfortable circumstances. On a farm eggs and potatoes, fruit and vegetables are usually dispensed with a liberal hand. We always have new milk for breakfast and cream on the supper table. Clothes do not interest me. They cost say–$5.00 a year. Certainly I am comfortable. But in one respect I am not comfortable–decidedly the reverse. All my life I have been giving money in tiny amounts to the poor; and now I have no money to give. My life has been long in the land and, generally as at present, on the land. Yes I have plenty to eat but money matters trouble me. There is my bruised and bleeding bank account, which, like a wounded snake drags its slow length along. If it should perish, where would I be, with not a cent to give the dear girl whose husband has a job today and next week it is like the grass, which today is, and tomorrow withereth away; not a nickel to bestow upon the jobless boy who owes his dentist a hundred dollars and who hates the telephones because the neighbours are always Johnny-on-the-spot when the collector calls; nothing but a spurious sympathy for the fine young fellow who pines for an education; naught but smooth words for the bed-ridden widow, whose frail daughter's salary is cut to the quick. How can I cast them off? I have a fatal gift of making friends and a large proportion of these friends are in circumstances worse than mine. My otherwise carefree leisure is beset by doubts and wonderings, of schemes and plans to help them if only a little.

In my heart of hearts I know I must make money, and give away money, else there is no peace for me in this life.

Ethelwyn Wetherald at age 80

THE PARTY
✧✧✧

It was 1938 when Ethelwyn intimated that she would like to have a party. This was very uncharacteristic of her, but perhaps she knew that she would not be on this earth much longer and longed to see some of her dearest friends before the time came to depart. She had so many friends as correspondents and many of them were more dear to her than would be our "best friend" of today. Having never met them she had her own picture of them as they were in spirit, not body. The one with the least in appearance could have been the very best in her mind's picture. She wrote dozens of letters each week and always looked forward to getting her mail each day. Most of them were far too far away to come to a party.

Her original intentions were to have the party at Tall Evergreens and I am sure that she was going to invite only her dearest friends for a quiet get-together, as was her style. Perhaps tea or coffee and some cookies, tarts etc. along with the beauty and peace of Tall Evergreens' country atmosphere. She could have had any kind of party and her friends would have loved it.

As it turned out, when she mentioned the party to Louis Blake Duff, he immediately took over and very kindly offered to host the whole party at his home, Cooneen Cross in St. John's. This was probably somewhat of a relief to Ethelwyn and I know she appreciated it, but at the same time she did want to greet her visitors "at home". It was decided to have everyone come to Tall Evergreens and then travel as a group to Cooneen Cross. This way she could enjoy her guests without worrying if everything had been done correctly. It worked out beautifully, although I feel that there were some guests without whom Ethelwyn could have been happier. She was a loving soul and wanted to have the people she felt closest to with her on this special occasion—to have little chats and probably relive some of the past. Guests must have been selected by both Louis Blake Duff and Ethelwyn, as it should have been, but I am sure the guest list would have had a different flavour had it been left entirely to Ethelwyn.

One of the guests appeared to be on a "promotional tour" as he insisted on reading some of his own poetry to the gathering—something Ethelwyn would have shrunk from had she been asked to read her poetry. However, Ethelwyn remained the perfect lady that she always was and played her part well.

Her hand-written invitation worded in her inimitable style was as follows:

Dear —
Would you add the charm of your presence to the anticipated fine weather of Saturday July 16, at the hour of three o'clock (DST) at Tall Evergreens, Fenwick and later at a picnic supper at Cooneen Cross, the home of Mr. and Mrs. Louis Blake Duff in St. John's.

RSVP   Ethelwyn Wetherald

Guests came from various places, near and far. Ethelwyn greeted them all, had them sign a guest book and made them more than welcome till the last person arrived. Then they took off in the motor convoy for Cooneen Cross.

It was about an eight-mile trek to Cooneen Cross, where Mr. and Mrs. Duff and their daughters Elizabeth and Patricia were waiting to greet everyone. The host and hostess were most gracious

Ethelwyn really should have worn what I term "the dress" to this party. She had a dress which she had worn back in the 1880s which was one of the most beautiful dresses I have ever seen. Long, of course, and with a bit of a bustle it had a deep hem of about twelve inches covered with pansies of most intense colours—blues, reds, maroons, yellows—just the way pansies really are. Pansies were sprinkled sparsely over the rest of the dress. The colours were just as vibrant as they would have been when new. It had been tucked away in a trunk when she came back to the farm to live and was taken out only when I begged to see it. Perhaps there was a story hidden in there. We will never know. It almost seems that she was playing the part of Cinderella when she returned to Tall Evergreens and put away her beautiful clothes never to wear them again. That dress would have been so colorful and although not in style, just right for the occasion of this party even though it was dated a half a century before.

A most pleasant afternoon was spent in the beautiful surroundings with a stream that one could almost call a river, running tight by the house. A new stone bridge had been built and Louis Blake Duff was more than happy to show all the visitors around his domain. Pictures were taken, food consumed and eventually everyone was ready to go home.

Back at home Ethelwyn was a very happy but very tired lady. She had had her party —her very last party—a party which must have brought back memories of people and places she had enjoyed long ago.

Scenes of the party at Cooneen Cross

THE DRESS

Ethelwyn Wetherald - 1939

1940

Ethelwyn Wetherald reads in front of fire at Tall Evergreens

It was March 1, 1940. A friend and I were going to a movie in the city, a distance of six miles. Kissing Nan goodbye, we started our walk to the car, which had been left at the highway, a mile away, because of deep snow. She was sitting happily at her little oval writing desk, reading *Gone With The Wind*. We knew that she would read until she was sleepy and then go to her bedroom. About a half mile from home we decided that the night was too stormy to go on—or was it Fate working? When we arrived home we found that Nan was very ill. She was put to bed under doctor's orders, but soon contracted pneumonia.

In the early morning of March 10th, 1940, Ethelwyn passed away. It was one of those piercingly still, bright, beautiful mornings with a fresh covering of snow on the ground, just waiting for the sun to rise and make the whole world sparkle— a morning which Ethelwyn would have enjoyed—a morning which would have inspired one of her beautiful poems. As she faced the unknown, the loving spirit which for so many years had embodied her still shone through as she uttered her last words to me: "I'm so glad I adopted you."

It was at the moment when the sun appeared over the horizon as a great ball of fire glistening on the virgin snow, that her great, gentle spirit took flight, leaving her legacy in her so frequently quoted poem:

LEGACIES

Unto my friends I give my thoughts,
Unto my God, my soul,
Unto my foe I leave my love —
These are of life the whole.

Nay, there is something— a trifle— left;
Who shall receive this dower?
See, Earth Mother, a handful of dust —
Turn it into a flower.

"Legacies" appeared in *The Last Robin* published in 1907 and also in *Lyrics and Sonnets* which was published in 1931. It was originally purchased by *Youth's Companion* and has been printed and quoted endlessly over the years.

Only a few short weeks before, in a letter to a friend, Elsie Pomeroy, dated December 26, 1939 Ethelwyn said:

"Living is a most enthusiastic process. This Christmas was one of the happiest periods of my life."

A published article written by Clara Bernhardt described the Christmas greeting Ethelwyn had sent her for the Christmas of 1939. On the card Ethelwyn had written:

> Be thine the sense of wings, the subtle call
> That comes from some bird-breasted waterfall;
> The comradeship of trees, the hearts of friends
> And one Near Presence where the footpath bends.

Ethelwyn also conveyed her feelings to Clara Bernhardt in a letter:

"I am divinely happy today partly because light came early this morning and will come earlier tomorrow. I am almost unnaturally well and feel correspondingly gay. I hope you too, are going on your way rejoicing."

Miss Bernhardt's comments were:

> On her way rejoicing! What a rare and admirable attitude for a solitary old lady of eighty-three! People half her age might well envy this spirit. It was through keeping alive her interest in the changing work and the younger generation, that Miss Wetherald retained her youthful outlook and verve. She wanted to know what the younger Canadian writers were doing. For in the letter she wrote me just a week before her death, was this adjuration: "Tell me about the younger poets with whom you feel in closest affinity. I am always interested."

Ethelwyn's funeral was held at her home Tall Evergreens, and burial took place at the Friends Cemetery, Pelham. As her family and friends turned to walk away from her grave, a beautiful white bird circled the mourners and then flew away almost as a tribute to what Ethelwyn stood for and what she gave others during her lifetime.

My own memories of Ethelwyn are her love, her warmth, her generosity, her caring for all people, her great sense of humour, her loyalty to family and friends even in great adversities, her fun-loving spirit, her understanding, and her ability to see beauty in everything.

THESE SHALL PERSIST

Whether I stir over the earth
    Or the earth stirs over me,
With weeds and flowers that come to birth
    After I cease to be.
Courage shall keep its worth,
    Truth shall make men free
Whether I move upon the earth
    Or the earth moves over me.
Whether I tread upon the grass
    Or the blades are green above,
Never from earth shall Beauty pass
    Nor joy from the eyes of Love,
Peace to the heart that grieves,
    To the toiler victory,
Whether I tread the drifting leaves
    Or the leaves drift over me.

The following, certainly the last poem Ethelwyn composed and shortly before her death, was written especially for the birthday of a dear friend Minnie Hallowell Bowen:

To Minnie Hallowell Bowen
on her birthday Feb. 4, 1940

> With thorns your soul is smitten,
> With unforgotten woes;
> But every thorn has written
> The autograph of a rose;
> Breath of a hazardous path rose-wreathed.

In an article, Clara Bernhart paid a tribute to Ethelwyn:

> Although "Legacies", which she once (jokingly) told me would be engraved upon her tombstone and "The Winds of Death" are probably her most widely known works, much of her work meets what she herself considered to be the final test of good poetry: It is worth reading aloud and worth memorizing. Only a week before her death, which occurred on March 10th, I received (from her) an autographed gift,, a copy of Page's Life of Homer Watson, accompanied by a gay letter requesting copies of my newest poems. She was, she said, divinely happy, because light was coming earlier now, and she was going her way rejoicing. Which is how I shall always think of Ethelwyn Wetherald—going her way rejoicing.

For many years, the tomb stone carried only the name Ethelwyn Wetherald as her descendants wished to do what they thought she preferred—no fuss, no publicity. When doing research on her life, the above article was found and the poem "Legacies" was promptly engraved on her stone in the Friends Cemetery in Pelham as her last message to all her friends and admirers.

A Selection of Poems

by

Ethelwyn Wetherald

POEMS

Green Boughs of Home	105
Untitled Poem	106
My Legacy	107
Give Me the Poorest Weed	107
Do You Remember	108
The Prayer of the Yer	109
The Indigo Bird	110
Beginning and End	111
A Wish	111
Homesickness	112
The Last Word	112
A March Night	113
An Old Influence	113
The Passing Year	114
The Roads of Old	115
Old Memories	116
Three Years Old	117
At Age 80	118
At Waking	118
Crosses and Kisses	119
Earth's Silences	120

The House of the Trees.................................. 121
The Red Winged Blackbird............................... 122
Stars and Flowers... 123
Every Common Day.. 123
The Question of Life.......................................124
The Hermit Thrsh...124
The Race...125
The Failure...125
The Woodlands Arms......................................126
Enchantment...126
To the Years...127
August Grass..127
Words..128
The Hummjngbird..129
What Love Remembers...................................129
Because Death Took You From Me....................130

GREEN BOUGHS OF HOME

Green boughs of home, that come between
Mine eyes and this far distant scene,
 I see, when e'er my thought escapes
Your old serene familiar shapes.

Each lissom willow tree that dips
Into the stream her golden whips,
The sassafras beside the gate,
Where twilight strollers linger late;

The hemlock groups that dimly hold
Their own against the noon-day gold,
The maple lines that give the view
A green or luminous avenue;

The oldest apple trees whose forms
Have braved a hundred years of storms,
And turn a face as blithe and free
To greet their second century;

The younger orchard's heavy edge,
Framed in the honey locust hedge;
Fruit-flushed, snow-burdened or bloom-bright,
It comes to my home-longing sight;

The billowy woods across the road
Where all the winds of heaven strode,
And sang in every towering stem,
Would that I were at home with them!

For under these down-bending boughs
A thousand tender memories house.
Oh, while your old companions roam,
Your peace be theirs, green boughs of home!

Untitled Poem

I shall not cry Return! Return!
Nor weep my years away
But just as long as sunsets burn
And dawns make no delay
I shall be lonely. I shall miss
Your hand, your voice, your smile, your kiss.

Not often shall I speak your name
For what would strangers care
That once a sudden tempest came
And swept my gardens bare
And then you passed and in your place
Stood silence with her lifted face.

Not always shall this parting be
For though I travel slow
I too may claim eternity
And go the way you go
And so I do my task and wait
The opening of the outer gate.

MY LEGACY

The little tree I planted out
    And often muse upon,
May be alive to grow and thrive
And out into the sunlight strive
    When I am dead and gone.

So it shall be my legacy
    To toilers in the sun.
So sweet its shade, each man and maid
May be induced to take a spade
    And plant another one.

GIVE ME THE POOREST WEED

Give me the poorest weed
To satisfy my spirit's need.
The brownest blade of grass
Will know and greet me when I pass.

Of their own feeling wrought,
They live like simple, vital thought;
The mind could not invent
A better thing than Nature sent.

DO YOU REMEMBER

Do you remember the drive we took
    Years ago, in the early fall,
When the moonlight lay like the visible look
    Of God, deep-brooding over all?

The prairie had broken into bloom
    Of golden-rod, like a web unrolled,
And there wasn't a tree to cast its gloom
    Over all that lustrous sweep of gold.

Never a house for miles and miles,
    Save our airy castles' columns and towers,
That rose in dimly magnificent piles
    Above a foundation of moonlit flowers.

We talked of our hopes and dreams, of how hard
    It was to live at the ideal height,
And our future was just as thickly starred
    As the sky above us that shining night.

Miles and miles through the loneliness
    A boy and a girl and a slow, slow steed,
The young hearts fluttering to express
    Their highest thought and their deepest need.

No hill of hardship, no vale of despair,
    But a golden plain and a golden sky,
We felt that life was thrillingly fair,
    And cared not to ask the reason why.

Ever so long ago, and we—
    How have we drifted each from each!
The road to the height where we longed to be
    Is all untraversed by smile or speech.

But still you remember that vanished year
    When we rode alone in the smile of God,
And all of our wealth on this mortal sphere
    Was poetry, youth and golden-rod.

THE PRAYER OF THE YEAR

Leave me Hope when I am old;
    Strip my joys from me,
Let November to the cold
    Bare each leafy tree;
Chill my lover, dull my friend,
    Only, while I grope
To the dark, the silent end,
    Leave me Hope!

Blight my bloom when I am old,
    Bid my sunlight cease;
If it need be, from my hold
    Take the hand of Peace.
Leave no springtime memory,
    But upon the slope
Of the days that are to be,
    Leave me Hope!

THE INDIGO BIRD

    When I see,
High on the tip-top twig of a tree,
Something blue by the breezes stirred,
But so far up that the blue is blurred,
So far up no green leaf flies
'Twixt its blue and the blue of the skies,
Then I know, ere a note be heard,
That is naught but the Indigo bird.

Blue on the branch and blue in the sky,
And naught between but the breezes high,
And naught so blue by the breezes stirred
As the deep, deep blue of the Indigo bird.

    When I hear
A song like a bird laugh, blithe and clear,
As though of some airy jest he had heard
The last and the most delightful word;
A laugh as fresh as the August haze
As it was in the full-voiced April days
Then I know that my heart is stirred
By the laugh-like song of the Indigo bird.

Joy on the branch and joy in the sky,
And naught between but the breezes high;
And naught so glad on the breezes heard
As the gay, gay note of the Indigo bird.

BEGINNING AND END

Once it was in my life's beginning,
    Roses were tall in their summer beds,
Dandelions within my fingers
    Thrust their confident golden heads;
Wading waist-deep amid the daisies,
    Feeling the grasses about me climb;
Thus it was in my life's beginning,—
    What have you done to me, Father Time?

So shall it be when life has ended;
    Roses shall bloom above my bed,
Dandelions will know I am lying
    Hidden in grass from foot to head.,
Hidden in grass and hidden in daisies,
    Over my breast I shall feel them climb;
Thus it will be when life has ended, —
    This will you do to me, Father Time.

A WISH

Life, like a wood-path, is a wavering
Love-shadowed, changeful beauty-haunted thing.
Some gleam of sun-gold dazzles and is gone;
Some fleeting, fawn-like rapture lures us on.
Be thine the sense of wings, the subtle call
That comes from some bird-breasted waterfall;
The comradeship of trees, the hearts of friends,
And one Near Presence where the footpath bends.

HOMESICKNESS

At twilight on this unfamiliar street,
    With its affronts to aching ear and eye,
    I think of restful fields that lie
Untrodden by a myriad fevered feet.
O green and dew and stillness!   O retreat
    Thick-leaved and squirrel-haunted! By and by
    I too shall follow all the thoughts that fly
Bird-like to you, and find you, ah, how sweet!

Not yet— not yet. To-night it almost seems
    That I am hasting up the hemlock lane
        Up to the door, the lamp, the face that pales
And warms with sudden joy. But these are dreams;
    I lean on Memory's breast, and she is fain
        To soothe my yearning with her tender tales.

THE LAST WORD

    Today when I heard you were dead,
    I remembered that you had said
    That death is the end of all.

    'Twas a long close argument
    We had—and my words were spent
    Like dew on a marble wall.

    You conquered my intellect quite.
    But— oh my comrade, to-night
    I know that you know I was right.

A MARCH NIGHT

A wild wind and a flying moon,
    And drifts that shrink and cower;
A heart that leaps at the thought, How soon
    The earth will be in flower.

Behind the gust and the ragged cloud
    And the sound of loosening floods,
I see young May with her fair head bowed,
    Walking in a world of buds.

AN OLD INFLUENCE

A child, I saw familiar things
    In sweet imagined guise;
For me the clouds were angels' wings
    The stars were angels' eyes.

Not so to-day; the grassless ways
    Of older years invite
No wings to whiten common days,
    No eyes to hallow night,

Yet when with grief my heart is loud,
    Or harsh thoughts leave their scar,
I feel reproach from every cloud,
    Reproof from every star.

THE PASSING YEAR

The feast is over, the guests are fled;
It is time to be old, it is time for bed.
The wind has blown out every light,
And the pleasure garden is turned to blight.
The trees like puffed-out candles stand,
And the smoke of their darkness is over the land.

    Heavily hangs the drowsy head,
        Heavily droop the lashes;
    To bed! To bed! Let prayers be said
        And cover the fire with ashes.

How the pipers piped, and the dancers flew,
Their hearts were piping and dancing too.
Wine of the sun and spell of the stream,
Birds in ecstasy, flowers that teem,
All gone by; now the quiet sky
Looks down on the earth where the snow must lie.

    Heavily hangs the drowsy head,
        Heavily droop the lashes;
    To bed! To bed! Let prayers be said
        And cover the fire with ashes.

THE ROADS OF OLD

The roads of old, how fair they gleamed;
How long each winding way was deemed.
    In days gone by, how wondrous high
Their little hills and houses seemed.

The morning road that led to school,
Was framed in dew that hung as cool
    To childish feet as waves that beat
About the sunbeams in a pool;

The river road, that crept beside
The dreamy alder-bordered tide,
    Where fish at play on Saturday
Left some young hopes ungratified;

The valley road, that wandered through
Twin vales and heard no wind that blew;
    The cowbell's clank from either bank
Was all the sound it ever knew;

The woodland road, whose windings dim
Were known to watchers straight and slim;
    How slow it moved, as if it loved
Each listening leaf and arching limb;

The market road that felt the charm
Of lights on many a sleepy farm,
    And whirring clocks and crowing cocks
Gave forth the market man's alarm;

The village road, that used to drop
Its daisies at the blacksmith shop,
    And leave some trace of rustic grace
To tempt the busiest eye to stop;

These all renew their golden spell.
With rocky cliff and sunny dell,
    With purling brook and grassy nook
They bordered childhood's country well.

And we who near them used to dwell
Can but the same sweet story tell,
    That on them went glad-eyed Content;
They bordered childhood's country well.

OLD MEMORIES

Old joy, old thrill, old loves
    Of faith serene and sure
Old tender tone, old bud half blown
    You shall endure.

Old trees, old books, old wine
    Old looks, old loves of mine
In the deep sky of days gone by
    Star-like you shine.

THREE YEARS OLD

What is it like, I wonder, to roam
    Down through the tall grass hidden quite?
To feel very far away from home
    When the dear house is out of sight?

To want to play with the broken moon
    In the star garden of the skies?
To sleep through twilight eves of June
    Beneath the sound of lullabies?

To hold up hurts for all to see,
    Sob at imaginary harms,
To clasp in welcome a father's knee,
    And fit so well to a mother's arms?

To have life bounded by one dull road
    A wood and a pond, and to feel no lack,
To gaze with pleasure upon a toad,
    And caress a mud-turtle's horny back?

To follow the robin's cheerful hop
    With all the salt small hands can hold,
And plead in vain for it to stop–
    What is it like to be three years old?

Ah, once I knew but 'twas long ago;
    I try to recall it in vain—in vain!
And now I know I shall never know
    What it is to be a child again.

AT AGE 80

Scores of glorious years behind me
And only a few small years before
I put out the candle and lock the door
 And take the place on the Heights assigned me.

But if there's naught to pity and cherish
Naught of striving, hoping and giving
In that strange new land of living
May my soul with my body perish.

AT WAKING

When I shall go to sleep and wake again
  At dawning in another world than this,
  What will atone to me for all I miss?
The light melodious footsteps of the rain,
 The press of leaves against my window pane,
  The sunset wistfulness and morning bliss,
  The moon's enchantment and the twilight kiss
Of winds that wander with me through the lane.

Will not my soul remember evermore
  The earthly winter's hunger for the spring,
   The wet sweet cheek of April and the rush
Of roses through the summer's open door;
  The feelings that the scented woodlands bring
    At evening with the singing of the thrush?

CROSSES AND KISSES

The letters I get from my little girl
    Are sure to end like this:
X   X   X   X   X   X   X
A score of crosses, row on row,
    And every cross is a kiss.
And through the miles that separate
    My own little one from me,
I feel the tug of her loving arms,
    And her loving face I see.

Every cross is a kiss, she says
    My crosses are never few,
They wait for me when I wake at morn,
    They follow the long day through.
I never dreamed they were sent in love—
    Ah me, what good I miss
When I push away with angry hands
    The cross that was meant for a kiss!

We mortals walk in a world of love,
    But we make it a world of care.
Some crosses are sharp and bring the blood,
    And some are heavy to bear.
But I think when we go in the arms of Death
    To heights of perfect bliss,
We shall see at a backward glance below
    That every cross was a kiss.

EARTH'S SILENCES

How dear to hearts by hurtful noises scarred
    The stillness of the many-leaved trees,
The quiet of green hills, the million-starred
    Tranquility of night, the endless seas
Of silence in deep wilds, where nature broods
In large, serene, uninterrupted moods.

Oh, but to work as orchards work—bring forth
    Pink bloom, green bud, red fruit and yellow leaf,
As noiselessly as gold proclaims its worth,
    Or as the pale blade turns to russet sheaf,
Or splendid sun goes down the glowing west,
Still as forgotten memories in the breast.

How without panting effort, painful word,
    Comes the enchanting miracle of snow,
Making a sleeping ocean. None have heard
    Its waves, its surf, its foam, its overflow;
For unto every heart, all hot and wild,
It seems to say, "Oh, hush thee! hush, my child!"

THE HOUSE OF THE TREES

Ope your doors and take me in,
    Spirit of the wood;
Wash me clean of dust and din,
    Clothe me in your mood.

Take me from the noisy light
    To the sunless peace,
Where at midday standeth Night,
    Signing Toil's release.

All your dusky twilight stores
    To my senses give;
Take me in and lock the doors,
    Show me how to live.

Lift your leafy roof for me,
    Part your yielding walls,
Let me wander lingeringly
    Through your scented halls.

Ope your doors and take me in,
    Spirit of the wood;
Take me—make me next of kin
    To your leafy brood.

THE RED WINGED BLACKBIRD

Black beneath as the night,
   With wings of a morning glow,
From his sooty throat three syllables float,
   Ravishing, liquid, low;
And 'tis oh, for the joy of June,
   And the bliss that ne'er can flee
From that exquisite call, with its sweet, sweet fall—
   O-ke-lee, o-ke-lee, o-kee-lee!

Long ago as a child,
   From the bough of a blossoming quince,
That melody came to thrill my frame,
   And whenever I've caught it since,
The spring-soft blue of the sky
   And the spring-bright bloom of the tree
Are a part of the strain—ah, hear it again!—
   O-ke-lee, o-ke-lee, o-ke-lee!

And the night is tenderly black,
   The morning eagerly bright,
For that old, old spring is blossoming
   In the soul and in the sight.
The red-winged blackbird brings
   My lost youth back to me,
When I hear in the swale, from a gray fence rail,
   O-ke-lee, o-ke-lee, o-ke-lee!

STARS AND FLOWERS

The stars enchant the upper skies
    The flowers chain the feet;
They look into each other's eyes,
    And flame and fragrance meet.
So will it be when Death unbars
    These slender doors of ours,
And turns our spirits into stars,
    Our bodies into flowers.

EVERY COMMON DAY

Every common day that we live is clasped and jeweled
    with love;
The stars of night are beneath it, the morning stars
    above.
The peace of God broods on it, as on her nest the
    bird
And over its weariest moments the music of hope
    is heard.

So, when my life-work is finished, and I go to God for
    my wage,
I wonder if He can give me a heavenlier
    heritage
Than to feel that each day that I live is clasped and
    jeweled with love,
With the stars of night beneath it and the morning
    stars above.

THE QUESTION OF LIFE

Would life give me soft airs, the dews of mirth
    The grapes of lover, the singing stars, the vast
Round joy of Summer, all the sweets of Earth
    And leave me at the last?

THE HERMIT THRUSH

A king would write a book of verse
    But how exceedingly hard
To be a titled genius
    Or even kingly bard.

But next door is a palace
    Whose crown and throne belong
To some leaf-hidden monarch
    A sovereign of song.

THE RACE

Life and Death ran a race
   Fleet on the wind:
Life went first a little space,
   Death close behind.

Life was crimson-lipped and gay,
   Suns on him shined;
Death was old, Death was gray—
   Still close behind.

Life slipped and lost his breath,
   Fell cold and blind—
Fell in the arms of Death,
   With God close behind.

THE FAILURE

A Failure, who had ne'er achieved
   Self victory, at last lay dead.
'Poor Failure'! Thus his neighbours grieved
   'Poor pitiable wretch,' they said,
'His weakness was the worst of crimes,
   He failed at least a thousand times'.

Meanwhile the Failure gave to God
   His vain attempts. Remorsefully
And prostrate on the skyey sod,
   'I failed a thousand times', said he.
'Welcome'! Rang out the heavenly chimes,
   'He strove—he strove a thousand times'!.

THE WOODLANDS ARMS

The woodlands arms to which I press
When the storm's sword their being cleaves
Still when the suns are pitiless
Encompass me with all their leaves.
So when my inner skies are rent
With blinding storms or cursed with heat,
These strong cool arms again are bent
To me and life once more is sweet.

ENCHANTMENT

Dearest, give your soul to me;
    Let it in your glances shine;
Let a path of ecstasy
    Stretch between your eyes and mine.
Should you press me to your heart,
    That enchanted,
That enchanted little pathway must depart.

Dearest, give your thoughts to me;
    Let them through the distance drear
Make unceasing melody
    To my raptured inner ear,
Should you clasp me—ah, the cost!
    All that elfin,
All that elfin music were in clamour lost.

TO THE YEARS

Take my youth then if your choose
      What care I?
Take the dawn and take the dews,
Not a rose tint I refuse,
Not a bird note shall I lose
      By and by
      You shall fly
In happy feet across the sky.

Take my life then if you will,
      What care I?
Break the cup and let it spill;
Though the wine run like a rill,
Till it fail and vanish, still
      By and by
      Life shall die
Full as ocean 'neath the sky.

AUGUST GRASS

Small rusty swords piled hundreds deep
      On Nature's battle ground,
With Peace beside them fast asleep
      In pasture fields are found.

Embattled Nature strives no more
      Her victory is won;
Her golden harvest trophies pour
      Their glory to the sun.

WORDS

I like those words that carry in their veins
    The blood of lions. "Liberty" is one,
    And "Justice," and the heart leaps to the sun
When the thrilled note of "Courage! Courage!"
       reigns
Upon the sorely stricken will. No pains
    Survive when "Life" and "Light," twin glories, run
    From the quick page to some poor soul undone,
And beggar by their glow all other gains.

How splendidly does "Morning" flood our night;
    How the word "Ocean" drowns our paltry cares,
        And drives a strong wind through our housed-
           up grief;
While "Honor" lifts us to the mountain height,
    And "Loyalty" the heaviest burden bears
        As lightly as a tree a crimson leaf.

THE HUMMING-BIRD

Against my window pane
    He plunges at a mass
Of buds—and strikes in vain
    The intervening glass.

O sprite of wings and fire
    Outstretching eagerly,
My soul, with like desire
    To probe thy mystery,

Comes close as breast to bloom,
    As bud to hot heart-beat,
And gains no inner room,
    And drains no hidden sweet.

WHAT LOVE REMEMBERS

What Love anticipates may die in flower,
What Love possesses may be thine an hour,
    But redly gleam in life's unlit Decembers
    What Love remembers.

BECAUSE DEATH TOOK YOU FROM ME

Because Death took you from me
I hear so much more clearly
The water dripping down the stones
We always loved so dearly.

Because Death took you from me
I feel you with me daily
Because you laughed so easily
I often laugh—and gaily.

Because Death took you from me
I walk your way, unsmothered
By Custom's small omnipotence
Nor do I go unbrothered.

Because Death took you from me
For all that once enchanted
Our roving thoughts, within my heart
Are now securely planted.

Books Written by Ethelwyn Wetherald
✦✦✦

An Algonquin Maiden: A Romance of the Early Days of Upper Canada. By Graeme
 Mercer Adam and A. Ethelwyn Wetherald. New York: J. Lovell, 1886; Montreal: J. Lovell, 1887; London: Low, Marston, Searle & Rivington, 1887; Toronto: Williamson, 887, c1886.

An Algonquin Maiden: A Romance of the Early Days of Upper Canada. By Graeme
 Mercer Adam and A. Ethelwyn Wetherald. (Reprint) Toronto: University of Toronto Press, 1973.

The House of the Trees and Other Poems. Boston; New York: Lamson, Wolffe,
 1895; Toronto: William Briggs, c1895.

Tangled in Stars. Boston: Richard G. Badger, 1902.

The Garden of the Heart: A Garland of Verses. By Ethelwyn Wetherald and Others.   Boston: Richard G. Badger, 1903.

The Radiant Road. Boston: Richard G. Badger, 1904
 c1903
The Last Robin: Lyrics and Sonnets. Toronto: William Briggs, 1907. Also published as *Poems, Lyrics and Sonnets.* Toronto: Musson.

Tree-Top Mornings. Boston: Cornhill, 1921.

Lyrics and Sonnets. Edited by John Garvin. Toronto: Thomas Nelson & Sons, 1931.